Alexandra's
GARDEN
VEGETABLES

ABOUT THE AUTHOR

Kerry Lord is the founder and creative director of the TOFT luxury yarn brand, which was established in September 2006. Kerry is the author of *Alexandra's Garden Flowers*, *Edward's Crochet Imaginarium*, *Edward's Crochet Doll Emporium*, *Edward's Menagerie: Dogs*, *Edward's Menagerie: The New Collection*, the 'How to Crochet Animals' series (*Farm/Pets/Wild/Ocean*) and *A Partridge in a Pear Tree*.

Pavilion
An imprint of HarperCollins*Publishers*
1 London Bridge Street
London SE1 9GF

www.harpercollins.co.uk

HarperCollins*Publishers*
Macken House
39/40 Mayor Street Upper
Dublin 1, D01 C9W8
Ireland

10 9 8 7 6 5 4 3 2

First published in Great Britain by Pavilion
An imprint of HarperCollins*Publishers* 2023

Publishing director: Stephanie Milner
Design director: Laura Russell
Senior designer: Alice Kennedy-Owen
Managing editor: Clare Double

A catalogue record of this book is available from the British Library

ISBN 978-0-00-855400-2

Printed and bound in Bosnia and Herzegovina

This book is produced from independently certified FSC™ paper to ensure responsible forest management.

For more information visit: www.harpercollins.co.uk/green

KERRY LORD

Alexandra's
GARDEN
VEGETABLES

30 CROCHET VEGETABLE PATTERNS

#alexsgarden
@toft_uk

PAVILION

Contents

The Projects   36

Introduction

Growing *Alexandra's Garden* has been an absolute pleasure from start to finish. It wasn't too long after I watched my first sunflower seed grow into a plant that was taller than me that I felt the urge to plant peas, beans and all types of other seeds in the ground – to fill our plates as well as our vases. My crochet garden was entirely a product of the pandemic years, when we all had to turn to our own four walls and the spaces right outside our homes to find inspiration and entertainment. Like many, in 2020 I found a new love for soil and a suspicion of slugs that I never could have predicted. My two young children came on this journey with me, which started with one sunflower seed and has ended with a very large vegetable patch! My real garden and my crochet garden grew symbiotically, inspiring each other every step of the way, and with far more learning curves and experimentation than I had ever had in the creation of a book before.

I've been trying to get five a day into my two children for a decade now, and never have I found that easier than when we have grown the vegetables ourselves, and especially if there is a larger-than-life crocheted counterpart to snuggle up with.

Crocheting and learning more about the vegetables in this book has also inspired three new deep and earthy colours in the TOFT yarn range. TOFT is a company I started in 2006, with no idea of what it would grow to become. Our vision is to enrich the lives of as many people as possible with our shared love of craft, and our mission is to be as creative and original as we can, making products to inspire creativity in others. We specialise in luxury natural yarns and long-lasting, high-quality tools that come together in your hands to give you pleasure as you savour the feeling of making the stitches, and spread happiness with the results of your time. With this book,

TOFT further expands our garden range, with an entirely new range of designs, colours and 100% compostable materials and tools.

When choosing where to begin with growing your crochet garden, consult the 'TIME TO GROW' description on each pattern to identify the smaller, faster projects. Quick-growing vegetables are projects that you'll be able to have on and off your hook in one evening, whereas slow projects are those that you might wish to return to over a longer period of making time.

I hope you enjoy cultivating these crochet patterns to create cute vegetables from the comfort of your sofa as much as I did when growing and eating their real counterparts!

Kerry Lord

How to use this book

The projects in this book are arranged seasonally throughout a year. Each project has a symbol (see below) indicating the skill level needed. Beginner projects will require only the basic stitches from pages 18–19, and easy and intermediate will require the advanced stitches on pages 24–25. If you're a complete newcomer to crochet, then start with the Practice Potato (page 34). I would then recommend the Courgette or Butternut Squash (pages 108 and 128) as brilliant first larger projects. Once you've made one of these you'll find it easy to progress on to whichever vegetable next takes your fancy, and learn a few new techniques along the way.

The vegetables have been designed with legs and arms as optional extras. You may opt to add both or none, or to pick and choose, as I've done throughout. The specific lengths and colours of limbs that I used are stated in each pattern. Standard limb patterns can be found on page 30.

If you're already a confident crocheter, dip in and out of the projects as you wish. Some designs use symbol charts for flat rather than 3D crochet pieces in addition to written instructions. If this is new to you, then refer to Reading a Chart on page 23.

All the stuffing and sewing-up guidelines are provided on the individual pattern pages, but more general tips about legs and arms can be found on page 30. Unless the pattern states otherwise, once you've worked the last round of each pattern piece, gather the stitches to fasten off using the technique detailed on page 30. All pieces can be stuffed at the end unless your pattern gives alternative instructions.

I've used British English crochet terms throughout. 'Double crochet' (dc) is the same as the American English 'single crochet' (sc). For clarification of all US terms and which stitches these refer to, see the table on page 24.

Skill level symbols

BEGINNER

EASY

INTERMEDIATE

Tools and materials

All the vegetables in this book are created using TOFT pure wool double knitting yarn on a 3mm hook with plant-based stuffing.

TOOLS

Hook

Choosing the right sized hook to match your yarn and create the correct tension is vital for ensuring the best results (see pages 16–17). If you're buying a hook for the first time, get a good-quality one with a comfortable handle as it will also double as the perfect tool for pushing the toy stuffing inside arms and legs!

Stitch marker

Marking the start or end of your rounds when working this style of crochet is essential. I recommend using a piece of contrast yarn, approximately 15cm long, positioned in the last stitch of Round 2 in any piece. As you return around to your marker, pull it forwards or backwards through or between your stitches to mark the end of the round you've just finished, to help keep track of where you are in the pattern. The marker will weave up the fabric with you, and you can pull it free at the end. Should you need to abandon your crochet halfway through a round, or if you lose your place when counting, you'll be able to return to your marker and avoid a total restart.

Scissors

Sharp scissors or thread snips are ideal for snipping off ends at the surface of the fabric once secured.

Stuffing

Several types of stuffing are available, including natural pure wool, plant-based 100% compostable fibres and recycled synthetic options. Using a recycled polyester stuffing will make your vegetables easier to wash by hand or in a cool cycle in the machine, and this tends to be a better option if they're being made as toys for children, whereas using all-natural materials guarantees that they're completely compostable!

Sewing needle

Choose a sewing needle with a big enough eye so that it's easy to thread with your yarn.

Contrast yarn or safety eyes

I used Cream and Black yarn to sew on the vegetables' eyes, and the same technique can be used to add a smile. Safety eyes can be added before sewing up, but they shouldn't be used on a toy for a child under five.

Row counter

Use a row counter if following a pattern is a new discipline for you. It may make it easier to keep track of the pattern if you don't wish to mark your place in the book.

Project bag

Although not essential, a project bag can be very handy for keeping your latest make safe and in order.

Pins for sewing up

If you're new to 3D crochet, pins might help you position all the parts before sewing them together. While not essential, they can come in handy if you know that sewing legs in straight lines poses a challenge for your perfectionism.

YARN

This collection of vegetable patterns inspired three new colours, which have now joined the TOFT range: Beetroot, Kale and Chive.

The quantity of yarn needed for these projects (based on TOFT pure wool double knit yarn) is stated in the table on the first page of each pattern. If using other brands of yarn, the quantities may vary significantly, depending on the fibre composition and spinning specifications. For example, a cotton yarn will be heavier and you'll require more of it, whereas an acrylic will be lighter and you'll

need less. See page 17 for the exact size of a standard vegetable leg made in TOFT double knitting pure wool.

You can use these patterns with thicker or thinner yarns and they will simply scale up or down to create bigger and smaller vegetables, but be aware that you'll require far more yarn for a bigger size – especially for larger projects like the pumpkin!

ABOUT TOFT

I've had the pleasure of selecting, designing and manufacturing luxury yarns since 2006 as the founder of the TOFT brand. TOFT yarns are luxury, high-quality natural fibres manufactured to my distinctive specifications here in the UK. When crocheted in TOFT yarns, the projects in this book are supple and soft but with a closed fabric to hide the stuffing inside. Using natural fibres is not only better for the environment, but also ensures a beautiful finish, assuring you that these vegetables will only get better over time, whether made for display or to play with, and guaranteeing each stitch is a pleasure to make.

TOFT is based in a real place called Toft – in Warwickshire, England – and we're always here to help if you're new to crochet and not sure where to begin. In addition to our yarns, TOFT now designs and manufactures a whole range of tools and accessories to accompany the Alexandra's Garden crochet range. Video help is also on hand if you're struggling at any point with the techniques in this book. All materials, kits and videos for these projects are available at www.toftuk.com.

Colours

Alexandra's Garden Vegetables has been created using a palette of five foliage colours, plus fifteen colours to cover all the edible roots, seeds, bulbs and fruits. On the first page of every project I recommend alternative colours to the ones I've shown, some of which might surprise you! I very much look forward to these vegetables and fruits being reimagined and crocheted into every other colour combination to create new species, and I'll continue to experiment with new combinations myself. The three new colours that were introduced to the TOFT yarn range – Beetroot, Chive and Kale – are deep, intensely earthy shades, and were essential additions to the palette to enable us to create a stunning rainbow of root vegetables.

Vegetables:
1. Cream
2. Cocoa
3. Oatmeal
4. Camel
5. Fudge
6. Chestnut
7. Mushroom
8. Yellow
9. Orange
10. Ruby
11. Magenta
12. Pink
13. Beetroot
14. Primrose
15. Amethyst

Foliage:
16. Green
17. Lime
18. Sage
19. Kale
20. Chive

Tension

The most important thing about making this style of stuffed crochet in double crochet stitch is to ensure that you're creating a closed fabric. If you're seeing holes in your fabric and subsequently stuffing through your stitches when working the patterns, swap your hook size down half a millimetre. Conversely, if your fabric is too solid and you're finding the stitches hard to work, then swap your hook size up half a millimetre. The leg shown opposite is the resulting size made using TOFT double knitting yarn and a 3mm hook. Use it to gauge your tension and adjust accordingly. If you find that this does not work, then take a look at the way you hold your hook and yarn and try to make a change to further impact your tension.

HOLDING YOUR HOOK

There are two principal ways of holding your crochet hook, one similar to holding a knife and the other to holding a pencil. If you're totally new to crochet, I'd recommend the knife hold as it's easier to get comfortable with, allowing you to maintain control and a good tension; if you already use the pencil hold successfully, then don't alter it. Even within these two holds there are lots of subtle variants on how to hold your hook – and there is no right or wrong way. Do what's most comfortable for you. If you're left-handed, there are no special changes you need to make as none of the patterns in this book refer to left or right. If it's necessary to clarify a direction of movement, I simply refer to your 'hook hand' and 'yarn hand'.

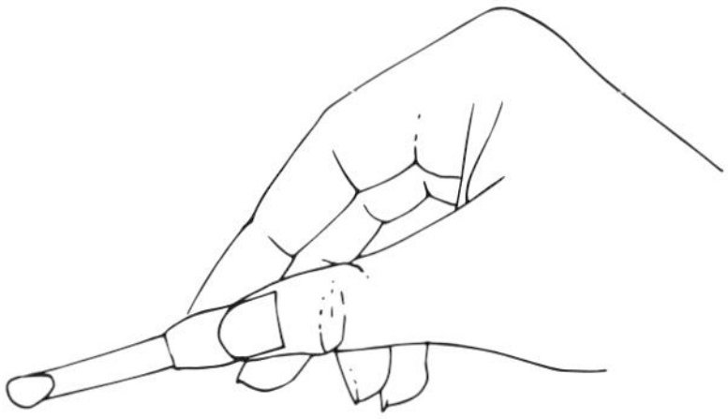

Knife hold

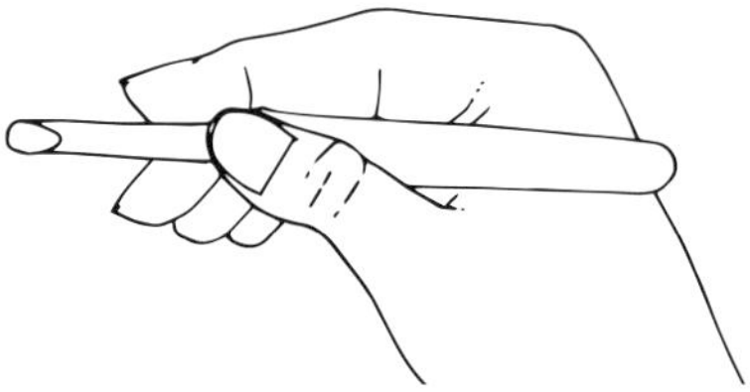

Pencil hold

HOLDING YOUR YARN

Every crocheter I meet holds their yarn in a slightly different way, so use the illustrations below as a rough guide and then experiment to find what's most comfortable for you. Only adjust your hand position if you think the way you hold the yarn is causing a problem. Loose stitches can be caused by not applying tension to the yarn coming off the ball by wrapping it around your finger, but the opposite problem – of the yarn not moving freely – can often be worse; you'll feel like you're fighting the stitches and creating a very tight tension.

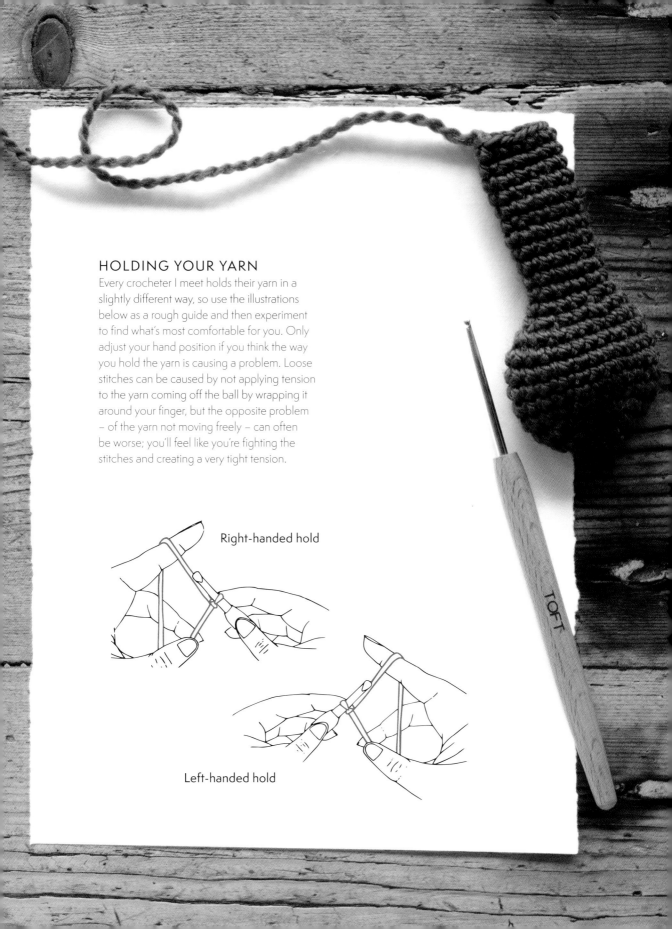

Right-handed hold

Left-handed hold

Learning to crochet (the basics)

Practise your hook and hand positions from the previous pages by working a long chain length. You'll get used to coordinating both hands and will find what works best for you. If you're managing to work the stitches and achieving the correct tension comfortably, then there's no right or wrong.

SLIP KNOT

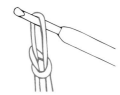

1   Wrap the yarn around your fingers.

2   Pull the tail end of the yarn through the wrap to make a loop.

3   Place your hook through the loop and tighten, ensuring that it's the tail end of the yarn (not the ball end) that controls the opening and closing of the knot.

CHAIN (CH)

1   Make a slipknot and place the loop on the hook.

2   Wrap the yarn over the hook (yarn over) and pull it through, keeping it close around the hook but not too tight.

3   Repeat until you reach the desired length (each repeat makes one chain).

DOUBLE CROCHET STITCH (DC)

1   Insert the hook through a stitch, under both loops of the 'V', unless stated otherwise.

2   Yarn over, rotate the hook head, and pull through the stitch (two loops on the hook).

3   Yarn over again and pull through both loops on the hook to end with one loop (one double crochet stitch made).

DC6 INTO RING (MAGIC CIRCLE)

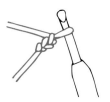 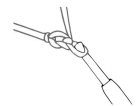 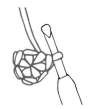

1   Make a slipknot and chain two stitches.

2   Insert the hook into the first chain stitch made and work a double crochet six times into this same stitch.

3   Pull tightly on the tail of the yarn to close the centre of the ring and form a neat circle.

DECREASING (DC2TOG)

 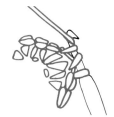 

1   Insert the hook under the front loop only of the next stitch (two loops on the hook).

2   In the same motion, insert the hook through the front loop only of the following stitch (three loops on the hook).

3   Yarn over and pull through the first two loops on the hook, then yarn over again and pull through both remaining loops to complete the double crochet decrease.

CHAIN AND THEN SL ST TO JOIN INTO A CIRCLE

  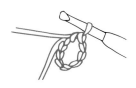

1   Chain the stated number of stitches, then insert the hook into the stitch closest to the slipknot, making sure you don't twist the stitches.

2   Yarn over the hook.

3   Pull the yarn through the stitch and the loop on the hook in one motion.

Counting your stitches

An essential skill for keeping yourself on track and able to follow a pattern accurately is knowing how to count the number of stitches you have in a round. While learning, count your stitches in a round after each line of pattern that involves increasing or decreasing. The number in parentheses at the end of a line of pattern indicates the number of stitches you should have once it's completed. If you complete a round and this number is wrong, then pull your work back to the beginning of the round and redo it until you have the correct number of stitches before you progress. This is much easier if you use a stitch marker (see page 10).

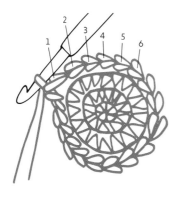

COUNTING THE STITCHES IN A ROUND

Your crochet piece will grow from a set number of stitches in a closed ring (usually six). The piece you're making then grows because you'll be instructed to increase the number of stitches by sometimes working two double crochet stitches into the same stitch.

When working the style of crochet used in this book to create a solid fabric and 3D shapes, you generally start from a closed ring and work the double crochet stitch in one direction in a non-stop spiral. The pattern for the start of the bodies for most of the vegetables forms a pretty standard increase for this style of crochet, adding six stitches evenly into every round. The piece becomes 3D once you stop adding six stitches into a round.

RIGHT SIDE (RS) AND WRONG SIDE (WS)

If you're new to this style of crochet you do need to be aware that there is a right side (RS) and wrong side (WS) to the fabric: the wrong side forms the inside of the shape. If you're right-handed and crocheting with the RS facing outwards, you'll be moving in an anti-clockwise direction around the edge of the circle of fabric (left-handed people will be moving clockwise). It's very easy to have learned to crochet holding the WS facing outwards (I did it myself); this will mean that your resulting piece is inside out when you come to stuff and finish it. With some parts this will not be a problem, as you can simply flip them before stuffing and sewing up. However, with the parts containing smaller rounds, such as the Parsnip stems, this will be impossible, so it's best to adjust your hold to ensure you're crocheting into the RS of the fabric, with the RS on the outside of the 3D shape. On the RS of the fabric you'll see the rounds horizontally on the piece. On the WS you'll see vertical furrows spiralling up the piece (see photos, right).

COUNTING A CHAIN

When you crochet a chain and then work back down it, you'll often miss the stitch closest to the hook in order to turn. For example, you might chain ten stitches in order to double crochet nine stitches back down the chain.

RS

WS

1
2
3
4
5
6

Reading a pattern

RND: ROUND
A round is a complete rotation in a spiral back to where you started. In this style of crochet you DO NOT slip stitch at the end of a round to make a circle, but instead continue directly onto the next round in a spiral.

DC: DOUBLE CROCHET
Dc2 means to double crochet one stitch into each of the following two stitches.

DC2TOG: DOUBLE CROCHET TWO TOGETHER
This is a decrease that reduces your stitch count by double crocheting into just the front of the next two stitches to turn them into one.

LEG

Begin by dc6 into ring

Rnd 1 (dc2 into next st) 6 times (12 sts)

Rnd 2 (dc1, dc2 into next st) 6 times (18)

Rnd 3 (dc2, dc2 into next st) 6 times (24)

Rnd 4 (dc3, dc2 into next st) 6 times (30)

Rnds 5–7 dc (3 rnds)

Rnd 8 (dc3, dc2tog) 3 times, dc15 (27)

Rnd 9 (dc2, dc2tog) 3 times, dc15 (24)

Rnd 10 (dc2tog) 12 times (12)

Rnds 11–23 dc (13 rnds)

Stuff end lightly and sew flat across top to close.

STS: STITCHES
The number in brackets at the end of a line indicates the number of stitches in that round once it has been completed.

6 TIMES
Repeat what comes directly before this instruction within the parentheses the number of times stated.

13 RNDS
Work one double crochet stitch into every stitch in the round for thirteen full rounds.

Reading a chart

Sometimes you'll find that a pattern includes a chart that you can use to help you visualise what you're making. Using the key below, follow the graphic from either the starting chain or the foundation ring. If crocheting left-handed, the chart would be worked as a mirror image of this. A new row or round will be indicated by a change of colour in the chart.

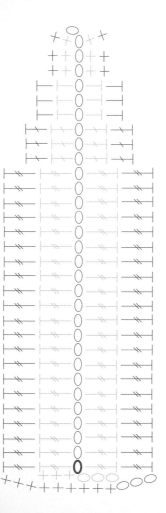

⊃	FOUNDATION RING (X STS INTO RING)
⬯	STARTING CHAIN
◯	CHAIN (CH)
●	SLIP STITCH (SL ST)
✛	DOUBLE CROCHET (DC)
⊤	HALF TREBLE CROCHET (HTR)
⊤	TREBLE CROCHET (TR)
⊤	DOUBLE TREBLE CROCHET (DTR)

Learning to crochet (advanced stitches)

Remember that this book uses British English crochet terms. See the key below for US equivalent terms.

UK		US	
ch	chain	ch	chain
sl st	slip stitch	sl st	slip stitch
dc	double crochet	sc	single crochet
dc2tog	dc 2 together	sc2tog	sc 2 together
htr	half treble crochet	hdc	half double crochet
tr	treble crochet	dc	double crochet
dtr (also ttr, qtr)	double treble crochet	tr	treble crochet
ttr	triple treble crochet	dtr	double treble crochet
qtr	quadruple treble crochet	ttr	triple treble crochet

HALF TREBLE CROCHET STITCH (HTR)

1 Yarn over and insert the hook into the next stitch.

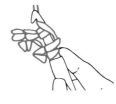

2 Yarn over and pull through the stitch (three loops on the hook).

3 Yarn over and pull through all three loops on the hook (one half treble crochet stitch made).

TREBLE CROCHET STITCH (TR)

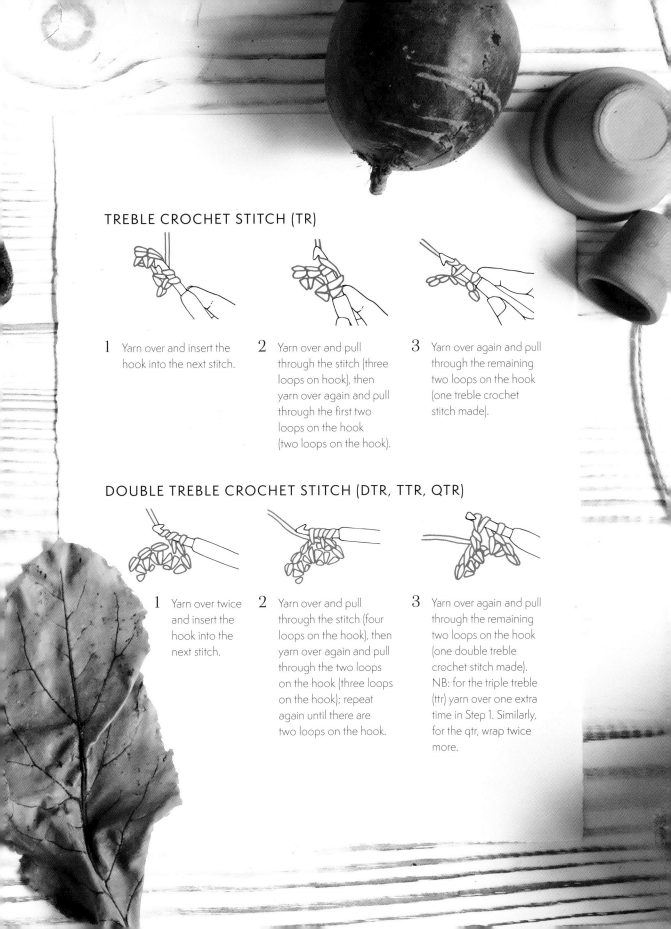

1 Yarn over and insert the hook into the next stitch.

2 Yarn over and pull through the stitch (three loops on hook), then yarn over again and pull through the first two loops on the hook (two loops on the hook).

3 Yarn over again and pull through the remaining two loops on the hook (one treble crochet stitch made).

DOUBLE TREBLE CROCHET STITCH (DTR, TTR, QTR)

1 Yarn over twice and insert the hook into the next stitch.

2 Yarn over and pull through the stitch (four loops on the hook), then yarn over again and pull through the two loops on the hook (three loops on the hook); repeat again until there are two loops on the hook.

3 Yarn over again and pull through the remaining two loops on the hook (one double treble crochet stitch made). NB: for the triple treble (ttr) yarn over one extra time in Step 1. Similarly, for the qtr, wrap twice more.

WORKING INTO BOTH SIDES OF A CHAIN TO START A ROUND

1 Chain the specified number of stitches.

2 Work the first stitch of the round into the second chain from the hook.

3 Continue working down the first side of the chain as instructed, then turn and work back up the other side of the chain to complete the first round. Place a marker.

COLOUR CHANGING

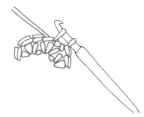

1 Insert the hook through the next stitch, yarn over and pull through the stitch (two loops on the hook).

2 Yarn over with the new colour and complete the double crochet stitch with this new yarn.

3 Continue with the new yarn, leaving the original yarn at the back of the work. Cut the original yarn if this is a one-off colour change, or run it along the back of the fabric if returning to it later.

BACK LOOP

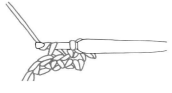

1 Insert the hook through the middle of the stitch to work the back loop only.

2 Yarn over and complete the stitch through this half of the stitch only.

3 Repeat to create a textured surface fabric as the front loops remain visible on the RS.

BOBBLE

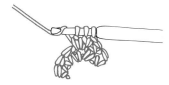 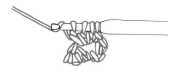

1 Yarn over and into the stitch. Now yarn over, bring back through the stitch, yarn over and back through two loops.

2 Repeat Steps 1 and 2 as many times as your pattern indicates.

3 Yarn over and into the stitch, yarn over, bring through the stitch, yarn over and pull through all the remaining loops on the hook.

WORKING FRONT POST/BACK POST

1 Yarn over, insert the hook around the post of the stitch below from front to back, pulling the post towards you. Complete st as indicated in the pattern (back post).

2 Yarn over, insert the hook around the post of the stitch below from back to front, pushing the post away from you. Complete st as indicated in the pattern (back post).

3 Using these two stitches alternately creates a deep rib.

CHAIN SPLIT

  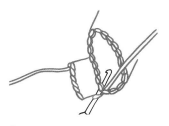

1 Chain the specified number of stitches from your current stitch. Insert the hook from the right side of the fabric through the specified stitch on the original round. This becomes Stitch 1 of the new round. Complete this round according to the pattern instructions.

2 Rejoin and work the main round as instructed.

3 Work stitches into the other side of the chain when you reach that point in the round.

Learning to crochet (finishing techniques)

JOINING TOGETHER WITH DC

1   Insert the hook through the edge of both pieces, ensuring the RS is facing outwards. The working direction is stated in your pattern; this determines which side the edge sits on.

2   Complete your stitch through both pieces of crochet.

3   Repeat until fully joined, making sure to stuff if instructed before the work is fully closed.

SLIP STITCH CHAINS

1   Insert the hook through the fabric at the desired position, yarn over and pull through the fabric.

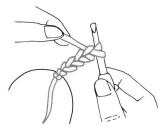

2   Chain the number of stitches stated in the pattern.

3   Work back down the chain. Insert the hook into each stitch, yarn over and pull through the stitch and loop until just one loop remains.

SLIP STITCH TRAVERSE

1   Insert the hook through the fabric at the desired position, yarn over and pull through the fabric.

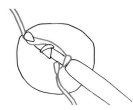

2   Repeat Step 1, moving across the surface of the fabric in the desired direction. Make sure you don't pull too tight, as this will result in puckering.

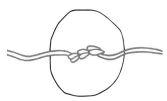

3   This can be used as a way of travelling across the fabric surface without having to break the yarn between slip stitch chains. These stitches may also be purely decorative.

MAKING LEAVES

Leaves are worked around a stem directly into the fabric between the rounds.
On many of the vegetable designs you'll be creating the leaves by crocheting longer
single-sided stitches directly onto a stem. Insert your hook in between the rounds of
the stem and slip stitch into place before following the pattern to create a series of
different-sized stitches. Adding two stitches into one space between the rounds will
cause the leaf to curl, so to create more natural-looking and less symmetrical leaves,
add in the odd stitch.

Stuffing and adding limbs

Once a part is complete, add the stuffing as instructed in that pattern, unless you've already been told to do so. The majority of parts will need to be finished by breaking the yarn, gathering the stitches and fastening off to enclose the stuffing, but others will require sewing flat or crocheting two pieces together.

GATHERING STITCHES

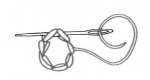

1 Fasten off the last stitch of the round by cutting the yarn and pulling the tail through the remaining loop.

2 Thread the end of the yarn onto a sewing needle and sew a running stitch through all the remaining stitches of the round.

3 Pull tightly to gather and close the stitches, then fasten off into the fabric around a stitch.

I've intended all the vegetables in this book to be made with optional limbs. Crochet the bodies and leaves without the arms and legs, and omit the eyes, and you'll have a perfect set of play food for any child's kitchen. Equally, they would also make a lovely interior display in a bowl or sitting on a dresser shelf in a kitchen. But if, like me, you enjoy creating a character, add legs and arms as you wish and sew them into position using the illustrations on pages 156–157 as a guide.

All of the feet and hands are stuffed, but the legs remain unstuffed. Once the stuffing is in place, sew the top closed either flat or perpendicular to the foot.

Straight leg

Perpendicular leg

Shaping

With a handful of the patterns, but most importantly with the Bell Pepper and the Pumpkin, the shape that you crochet is only realised in vegetable form once you stuff and invert the ends by sewing them through the centre of the piece. Once your stuffing is in, gather all the final stitches to close and invert both the top and the bottom by sewing directly down through the centre of the shape, then back up through to the top again, pulling tight before securing the end.

Adding eyes

I embroidered eyes on all of the vegetables using TOFT DK yarn in Cream and Black.

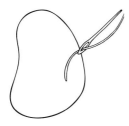  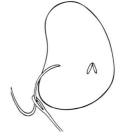

1 Secure Cream yarn at the top of the desired eye position.

2 Sew into the fabric three rounds down (or four, if making very large vegetables, such as the Pumpkin), one stitch across and back down into the original hole.

3 Complete the triangle shape in Cream and fasten off.

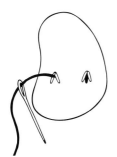

4 Using Black, sew two wraps in the centre of the triangle.

If you want to use safety eyes, don't forget to add them before gathering the stitches on the body. This can be a little fiddly as you'll need to push them through the fabric and then reach up through the body to secure the backs before stuffing and closing the whole part. You don't need to add eyes to your vegetables, but equally, you might want to consider creating some additional features such as mouths, as I've done on some of them. The Peas in a Pod are perfect for mastering this technique – try to create a different expression on each pea using just a few embroidered stitches in Black.

Practice potato

If you're new to crochet, or you'd simply like a warm-up, try this little chitting potato to master all the basic techniques as well as a couple of others – plus your first set of embroidered eyes. If you can master this then you'll be ready to make any of the 'BEGINNER' vegetables.

YOU WILL NEED

25g of one colour of double knitting wool and a scrap of contrast for the shoots (shown here are Oatmeal and Cream), plus a 3mm hook

BODY

The body is worked from the top down.
Working in Oatmeal
Begin by dc6 into ring
Rnd 1 (dc2 into next st) 6 times (12 sts)
Rnd 2 (dc1, dc2 into next st) 6 times (18)
Rnd 3 (dc2, dc2 into next st) 6 times (24)
Rnd 4 dc
Rnd 5 (dc3, dc2 into next st) 6 times (30)
Rnds 6–8 dc (3 rnds)
Rnd 9 (dc3, dc2tog) 3 times, (dc4, dc2 into next st) 3 times (30)
Rnd 10 dc12, (dc5, dc2 into next st) 3 times (33)
Rnd 11 dc12, (dc6, dc2 into next st) 3 times (36)
Rnds 12–16 dc (5 rnds)
Rnd 17 (dc11, dc2 into next st) 3 times (39)
Rnd 18 dc
Rnd 19 (dc11, dc2tog) 3 times (36)
Rnd 20 (dc4, dc2tog) 6 times (30)
Rnd 21 (dc3, dc2tog) 6 times (24)
Rnd 22 (dc2, dc2tog) 6 times (18)
Rnd 23 (dc1, dc2tog) 6 times (12)
Rnd 24 (dc2, dc2tog) 3 times (9)
Stuff body and gather final stitches to close.

SHOOTS

Work as many shoots as you would like onto the body.
Working in Cream
Sl st into position, ch7, turn and work back down chain as follows:
sl st3, dc2 into next st, dc2, sl st into body
*Ch5, turn and work back down chain as follows:
sl st2, dc2 into next st, dc1, sl st into body
Repeat from * once more
Break yarn.

Embroider eyes with Black and Cream yarn, and mouth with Black yarn.

The
PROJECTS

Carrot

The most iconic of the root vegetables is available in a wide range of rainbow varieties. This pattern is so fun and simple that you'll want to make a whole bunch in different colours. The old wisdom about the benefits of carrots for your eyesight also make this the perfect comforting bedfellow for any little person afraid of the dark.

BODY

The body is worked from the top down.
Working in Orange
Begin by dc6 into ring
Rnd 1 (dc2 into next st) 6 times (12 sts)
Rnd 2 (dc1, dc2 into next st) 6 times (18)
Rnd 3 (dc2, dc2 into next st) 6 times (24)
Rnd 4 (dc3, dc2 into next st) 6 times (30)
Rnd 5 (dc4, dc2 into next st) 6 times (36)
Rnd 6 (dc5, dc2 into next st) 6 times (42)
Rnds 7–21 dc (15 rnds)
Rnd 22 (dc5, dc2tog) 6 times (36)
Rnds 23–35 dc (13 rnds)
Rnd 36 (dc2tog, dc10) 3 times (33)
Rnd 37 dc
Rnd 38 (dc2tog, dc9) 3 times (30)
Rnd 39 dc
Rnd 40 (dc2tog, dc8) 3 times (27)
Rnd 41 dc
Rnd 42 (dc2tog, dc7) 3 times (24)
Rnd 43 dc
Rnd 44 (dc2tog, dc6) 3 times (21)
Rnd 45 dc
Rnd 46 (dc2tog, dc5) 3 times (18)
Rnd 47 dc
Rnd 48 (dc4, dc2tog) 3 times (15)
Rnd 49 dc
Rnd 50 (dc3, dc2tog) 3 times (12)

Stuff and continue
Rnd 51 (dc2, dc2tog) 3 times (9)
Rnd 52 (dc1, dc2tog) 3 times (6)
Rnd 53 dc

LEAVES

Working in Lime
Make STEMS and then work LEAVES around edge of each STEM.

SHORT STEM (make two)

Begin by dc6 into ring
Rnds 1–28 dc (28 rnds)
Break yarn.

LONG STEM (make one)

Begin by dc6 into ring
Rnds 1–38 dc (38 rnds)
Break yarn.

LEAVES

Sl st into position 16 rnds down stem and then work along stem towards top as follows:
*ch9, turn and work back down chain as follows:
sl st1, dc1, htr1, tr5
miss 2 sts and SLIP STITCH TRAVERSE (see page 28) 2 sts along stem
Continues overleaf

MADE IN Orange and Lime (overleaf in Orange and Yellow with Green foliage)
YARN QUANTITIES 50g Vegetable, 50g Foliage
TIME TO GROW Moderate
REQUIRES htr, tr, slip stitch traverse

Repeat from * along stem towards top,
   work one into top and then continue
   down opposite side.

LEGS (make two)
Working in Lime
Begin by dc6 into ring
Rnd 1 (dc2 into next st) 6 times (12)
Rnd 2 (dc1, dc2 into next st) 6 times (18)
Rnd 3 (dc2, dc2 into next st) 6 times (24)
Rnd 4 (dc3, dc2 into next st) 6 times (30)
Rnds 5–7 dc (3 rnds)
Rnd 8 (dc3, dc2tog) 3 times, dc15 (27)
Rnd 9 (dc2, dc2tog) 3 times, dc15 (24)
Rnd 10 (dc2tog) 12 times (12)
Rnds 11–28 dc (18 rnds)

SEWING UP
1. Gather final stitches of BODY to close.
2. Stuff feet and sew tops of LEGS flat
   perpendicular to foot and sew into position
   on sides of BODY.
3. Sew in all ends and then sew the three
   LEAVES together at the tips, with the long
   leaf in the middle.
4. Sew LEAVES onto top of BODY.
5. Embroider eyes with Black and Cream yarn.

Button Mushroom

A really cute little crochet project and a delicious edible mushroom that's a staple ingredient in so many dishes, from bolognese to stirfries. Why not hook up a whole troop of little white caps in all sizes, using different thicknesses of yarn, to bring a smile to any cook's kitchen?

CAP

Working in Cream
Begin by dc6 into ring
Rnd 1 (dc2 into next st) 6 times (12 sts)
Rnd 2 (dc1, dc2 into next st) 6 times (18)
Rnd 3 (dc2, dc2 into next st) 6 times (24)
Rnd 4 (dc3, dc2 into next st) 6 times (30)
Rnd 5 (dc4, dc2 into next st) 6 times (36)
Rnd 6 (dc5, dc2 into next st) 6 times (42)
Rnd 7 (dc6, dc2 into next st) 6 times (48)
Rnd 8 (dc7, dc2 into next st) 6 times (54)
Rnd 9 dc
Rnd 10 (dc8, dc2 into next st) 6 times (60)
Rnds 11–13 dc (3 rnds)
Rnd 14 (dc9, dc2 into next st) 6 times (66)
Rnds 15–17 dc (3 rnds)
Rnd 18 (dc9, dc2tog) 6 times (60)
Rnd 19 (dc8, dc2tog) 6 times (54)
Change to Mushroom
Rnd 20 (dc7, dc2tog) 6 times (48)
Rnd 21 (dc2, dc2tog) 12 times (36)
Rnd 22 (dc2tog) 18 times (18)
Rnd 23 (dc1, dc2tog) 6 times (12)
Rnd 24 (dc2, dc2tog) 3 times (9)

STEM

Working in Cream
Ch30 and sl st to join into a circle
Rnds 1–6 dc (6 rnds)

Change to Mushroom
Rnd 7 dc
Rnd 8 (ch3, sl st1 into next st) 30 times
Break yarn.

BASE

Working in Cream
Begin by dc6 into ring
Rnd 1 (dc2 into next st) 6 times (12 sts)
Rnd 2 (dc1, dc2 into next st) 6 times (18)
Rnd 3 (dc2, dc2 into next st) 6 times (24)
Rnd 4 (dc3, dc2 into next st) 6 times (30)
Break yarn.

SEWING UP

1. Stuff CAP and gather stitches to close.
2. Sew STEM into position on bottom of CAP using colour change line as a guide.
3. Stuff STEM and join BASE with a round of dc from the bottom up in Cream.
4. Stuff feet and sew top of LEGS flat, then sew into position on joining edge of BASE.
5. Embroider eyes with Black and Cream yarn, and mouth with Black yarn.

MADE IN Cream and Mushroom
YARN QUANTITIES 25g Cap, 25g Contrast
TIME TO GROW Quick
REQUIRES Colour change

Beetroot

Beetroot juice has been used as a red dye in textile manufacturing for centuries, and it was even used as a hair dye in the Victorian era! It's an easy vegetable to grow in any garden, and very versatile – eaten raw, roasted, pickled, steamed or even baked in cakes.

BODY
The body is worked from the top down.
Working in Beetroot
Begin by dc6 into ring
Rnd 1 (dc2 into next st) 6 times (12 sts)
Rnd 2 (dc1, dc2 into next st) 6 times (18)
Rnd 3 (dc2, dc2 into next st) 6 times (24)
Rnd 4 (dc3, dc2 into next st) 6 times (30)
Rnd 5 (dc4, dc2 into next st) 6 times (36)
Rnd 6 (dc5, dc2 into next st) 6 times (42)
Rnd 7 (dc6, dc2 into next st) 6 times (48)
Rnd 8 dc
Rnd 9 (dc7, dc2 into next st) 6 times (54)
Rnd 10 dc
Rnd 11 (dc8, dc2 into next st) 6 times (60)
Rnds 12–21 dc (10 rnds)
Rnd 22 (dc4, dc2tog) 10 times (50)
Rnd 23 (dc3, dc2tog) 10 times (40)
Rnd 24 (dc2, dc2tog) 10 times (30)
Rnd 25 dc
Rnd 26 (dc8, dc2tog) 3 times (27)
Rnd 27 (dc7, dc2tog) 3 times (24)
Rnd 28 (dc2, dc2tog) 6 times (18)
Rnd 29 dc
Rnd 30 (dc2tog) 9 times (9)
Stuff and continue
Rnds 31–32 dc (2 rnds)
Rnd 33 (dc1, dc2tog) 3 times (6)
Rnd 34 dc
Rnd 35 (dc1, dc2tog) twice (4)
Ch5, turn and work back down chain
    as follows:
sl st2, dc2, sl st into end

LEAVES
Make STEMS and then work LEAVES around
    edge of each STEM.

STEM (make two)
Working in Beetroot
Begin by dc6 into ring
Rnds 1–28 dc (28 rnds)
Break yarn.

LEAVES
Working in Green
Sl st into position 18 rnds down stem
    and then work along stem towards top
    as follows:
ch3, (dtr1, ttr2, dtr1, tr1) 3 times, dtr1, ttr2
    into next st
ttr6 into top of stem and then continue to
    work down other side as follows:
ttr2 into next st, dtr1, (tr1, dtr1, ttr2, dtr)
    3 times, tr1
Break yarn.

Continues overleaf

MADE IN Beetroot, Green and Lime (overleaf in Magenta)
YARN QUANTITIES 50g Vegetable, 25g Foliage, 25g Legs
TIME TO GROW Quick
REQUIRES tr, dtr, ttr

Rejoin at the top of starting chain and then
    work around edge as follows:
dc16, (dc2 into next st) 10 times, dc17
Break yarn.

LEGS (make two)
Working in Lime
Begin by dc6 into ring
Rnd 1 (dc2 into next st) 6 times (12)
Rnd 2 (dc1, dc2 into next st) 6 times (18)
Rnd 3 (dc2, dc2 into next st) 6 times (24)
Rnd 4 (dc3, dc2 into next st) 6 times (30)
Rnds 5–7 dc (3 rnds)
Rnd 8 (dc3, dc2tog) 3 times, dc15 (27)

Rnd 9 (dc2, dc2tog) 3 times, dc15 (24)
Rnd 10 (dc2tog) 12 times (12)
Rnds 11–28 dc (18 rnds)

SEWING UP
1. Sew in all ends on LEAVES, then sew two
    LEAVES together at bottom.
2. Sew LEAVES into position on top of BODY.
3. Stuff feet and sew tops of LEGS flat
    perpendicular to foot, then sew into position
    on bottom of BODY.
4. Embroider eyes with Black and Cream yarn.

Leek

The national emblem of Wales, the leek is a much-loved vegetable, traditionally combined with potatoes in everything from stews and soups to pasties and pies. Cultivated for thousands of years, it has a long and rich cultural history globally, dating back to the Egyptians and the Romans.

BODY

The body is worked from the bottom up.
Working in Cream
Begin by dc6 into ring
Rnd 1 (dc2 into next st) 6 times (12 sts)
Rnd 2 (dc1, dc2 into next st) 6 times (18)
Rnd 3 (dc2, dc2 into next st) 6 times (24)
Rnd 4 (dc3, dc2 into next st) 6 times (30)
Rnd 5 (dc4, dc2 into next st) 6 times (36)
Rnd 6 (dc5, dc2 into next st) 6 times (42)
Rnd 7 (dc6, dc2 into next st) 6 times (48)
Rnd 8 dc
Rnd 9 (dc6, dc2tog) 6 times (42)
Rnds 10–13 dc (4 rnds)
Rnd 14 (dc2tog, dc12) 3 times (39)
Rnds 15–18 dc (4 rnds)
Rnd 19 (dc2tog, dc11) 3 times (36)
Rnds 20–27 dc (8 rnds)
Change to Chive
Rnds 28–31 dc (4 rnds)
Rnd 32 (dc2tog, dc10) 3 times (33)
Rnds 33–42 dc (10 rnds)
Rnd 43 (dc2 into next st, dc10) 3 times (36)
Rnd 44 (dc5, dc2 into next st) 6 times (42)
dc1, ch14, count 14 sts back on rnd and sl st to
   create a 28-st round. Work as follows:
Rnds 1–14 dc (14 rnds)

Rejoin and work main 42-st rnd as follows:

(28 sts from rnd, 14 sts from chain)
Rnds 1–4 dc (4 rnds)

Dc20, ch14, count 14 sts back on rnd and sl st
   to create a 28–st round. Work as follows:
Rnds 1–12 dc (12 rnds)

Rejoin and work main 42-st rnd as follows:
Rnds 1–2 dc (2 rnds)

Dc8, ch14, count 14 sts back on rnd and sl st to
   create a 28-st round. Work as follows:
Rnds 1–10 dc (10 rnds)

Rejoin and dc20, ch14, count 14 sts back on
   rnd and sl st to create a 28-st round. Work
   as follows:
Rnds 1–8 dc (8 rnds)

Rejoin and work main 42-st rnd as follows:
Rnd 1 (dc5, dc2tog) 6 times (36)
Rnds 2–7 dc (6 rnds)
Break yarn and stuff the central stem.

ROOTS

Working in Cream
Sl st into position on bottom of BODY approx.
   4 rnds out from starting ring
Continues overleaf

MADE IN Cream and Chive (overleaf in Lime and Green – change after Rnd 39)
YARN QUANTITIES 50g Main, 50g Leaves
TIME TO GROW Slow
REQUIRES Chain split, slip stitch traverse, colour change

*Ch9, turn and work back down chain as
  follows:
sl st3, dc2 into next ch, dc4
SLIP STITCH TRAVERSE (see page 28) 3 sts
  around rnd and then repeat from * five
  more times

TOP
Working in Chive
Begin by dc6 into ring
Rnd 1 (dc2 into next st) 6 times (12)
Rnd 2 (dc1, dc2 into next st) 6 times (18)
Rnd 3 (dc2, dc2 into next st) 6 times (24)
Rnd 4 (dc3, dc2 into next st) 6 times (30)
Rnd 5 (dc4, dc2 into next st) 6 times (36)
Break yarn.

Working in Cream
Work a spiral of SLIP STITCH TRAVERSE onto
  TOP, ensuring that you are working with right
  side facing.

LEGS (make two)
Working in Cream
Begin by dc6 into ring
Rnd 1 (dc2 into next st) 6 times (12)
Rnd 2 (dc1, dc2 into next st) 6 times (18)
Rnd 3 (dc2, dc2 into next st) 6 times (24)
Rnd 4 (dc3, dc2 into next st) 6 times (30)
Rnds 5–7 dc (3 rnds)

Rnd 8 (dc3, dc2tog) 3 times, dc15 (27)
Rnd 9 (dc2, dc2tog) 3 times, dc15 (24)
Rnd 10 (dc2tog) 12 times (12)
Rnds 11–18 dc (8 rnds)

ARMS (make two)
Working in Cream
Begin by dc6 into ring
Rnd 1 (dc2 into next st) 6 times (12)
Rnd 2 (dc1, dc2 into next st) 6 times (18)
Rnd 3 (dc2, dc2 into next st) 6 times (24)
Rnds 4–8 dc (5 rnds)
Rnd 9 dc6, (dc1, dc2tog) 6 times (18)
Rnd 10 dc6, (dc2tog) 6 times (12)
Rnds 11–22 dc (12 rnds)

SEWING UP
1. Attach TOP to top of central stem with a
   round of dc from the top down.
2. Fold each outside leaf layer flat and dc
   across top to close.
3. Stuff feet and sew tops of LEGS flat
   perpendicular to foot, then sew into position
   on bottom of BODY.
4. Stuff hands and sew tops of ARMS flat
   perpendicular to hand, then sew into
   position on sides of BODY.
5. Embroider eyes with Black and Cream yarn.

Curly Kale

Kale belongs to the same family as cabbage and Brussels sprouts, and is a powerhouse of minerals and vitamins and those all-important antioxidants. Much like the real thing, this is an easy yet slow-growing vegetable, with a high stitch count to create those stunning curly leaves.

BODY
The body is worked from the bottom up.
Working in Sage
Ch30 and sl st to join into a circle
Rnds 1–6 dc (6 rnds)
Rnd 7 (dc8, dc2tog) 3 times (27)
Rnds 8–13 dc (6 rnds)
Rnd 14 (dc7, dc2tog) 3 times (24)
Rnds 15–18 dc (4 rnds)
Rnd 19 (dc6, dc2tog) 3 times (21)
Rnds 20–23 dc (4 rnds)
Rnd 24 (dc5, dc2tog) 3 times (18)
Rnds 25–28 dc (4 rnds)
Rnd 29 (dc4, dc2tog) 3 times (15)
Rnds 30–33 dc (4 rnds)
Rnd 34 (dc3, dc2tog) 3 times (12)
Rnds 35–38 dc (4 rnds)
Rnd 39 (dc2, dc2tog) 3 times (9)
Rnds 40–43 dc (4 rnds)
Rnd 44 (dc1, dc2tog) 3 times (6)
Rnd 45 dc
Dc3 through both sides to close
Ch6, turn and work back down chain as
    follows:
sl st2, dc1, htr2, sl st into body to secure.

BASE
Working in Sage
Begin by dc6 into ring

Rnd 1 (dc2 into next st) 6 times (12)
Rnd 2 (dc1, dc2 into next st) 6 times (18)
Rnd 3 (dc2, dc2 into next st) 6 times (24)
Rnd 4 (dc3, dc2 into next st) 6 times (30)
Break yarn.

LEAVES (make two)
Working in Kale
Begin by dc6 into ring
Rnd 1 (dc2 into next st) 6 times (12)
Rnd 2 (dc1, dc2 into next st) 6 times (18)
Rnd 3 (dc2, dc2 into next st) 6 times (24)
Rnd 4 (dc3, dc2 into next st) 6 times (30)
Rnd 5 (dc4, dc2 into next st) 6 times (36)
Rnd 6 (dc5, dc2 into next st) 6 times (42)
Rnd 7 (dc6, dc2 into next st) 6 times (48)
Rnd 8 (dc7, dc2 into next st) 6 times (54)
Rnd 9 (dc8, dc2 into next st) 6 times (60)
Rnd 10 (dc9, dc2 into next st) 6 times (66)
Rnd 11 (dc10, dc2 into next st) 6 times (72)
Rnd 12 (dc11, dc2 into next st) 3 times,
    (dc2 into next st) 36 times (111)
Rnd 13 (dc12, dc2 into next st) 3 times,
    (dc2 into next st) 72 times (186)
Rnd 14 (dc13, dc2 into next st) 3 times,
    (dc2 into next st) 144 times (333)
Fold in half symmetrically and dc22 through
    both sides of the non-frilled section to close.
Continues overleaf

MADE IN Kale and Sage (overleaf in Green and Lime)
YARN QUANTITIES 50g Body, 50g Leaf
TIME TO GROW Slow
REQUIRES htr

Turn and work in rows as follows:
Row 1 (dc3 into next st) 22 times (66)
Row 2 (dc2 into next st) 66 times (132)

LEGS (make two)
Working in Sage
Begin by dc6 into ring
Rnd 1 (dc2 into next st) 6 times (12)
Rnd 2 (dc1, dc2 into next st) 6 times (18)
Rnd 3 (dc2, dc2 into next st) 6 times (24)
Rnd 4 (dc3, dc2 into next st) 6 times (30)
Rnds 5–7 dc (3 rnds)
Rnd 8 (dc3, dc2tog) 3 times, dc15 (27)
Rnd 9 (dc2, dc2tog) 3 times, dc15 (24)
Rnd 10 (dc2tog) 12 times (12)
Rnds 11–18 dc (8 rnds)

ARMS (make two)
Working in Sage
Begin by dc6 into ring
Rnd 1 (dc2 into next st) 6 times (12)
Rnd 2 (dc1, dc2 into next st) 6 times (18)
Rnd 3 (dc2, dc2 into next st) 6 times (24)
Rnds 4–8 dc (5 rnds)
Rnd 9 dc6, (dc1, dc2tog) 6 times (18)
Rnd 10 dc6, (dc2tog) 6 times (12)
Rnds 11–22 dc (12 rnds)

VEINS
Working in Sage

TOP (make two)
Ch5, turn and work back down chain as
    follows:
sl st1, dc1, htr2, break yarn.

MIDDLE (make two)
Ch7, turn and work back down chain as follows:
sl st1, dc1, htr4, break yarn.

BOTTOM (make two)
Ch9, turn and work back down chain as
    follows:
sl st1, dc1, htr6, break yarn.

SEWING UP
1. Stuff BODY and join BASE with a round of dc
   from the top down in Sage.
2. Sew LEAVES into position on sides of BODY
   with open section of frill at top.
3. Sew VEINS into position using photos as
   a guide.
4. Stuff feet and sew top of LEGS flat, then sew
   into position on joining edge of BASE.
5. Stuff hands and sew tops of ARMS flat
   perpendicular to hand, then sew into
   position on sides of BODY.
6. Embroider eyes with Black and Cream yarn.

Parsnip

Staple of the traditional Sunday roast, these sweet root vegetables only get better if exposed to low temperatures, as more starch converts to sugar with each frost. This is an easy pattern that you can customise to be as gnarly as you wish, with the addition of the slip stitched surface texture.

BODY
The body is worked from the top down.
Working in Oatmeal
Begin by dc6 into ring
Rnd 1 (dc2 into next st) 6 times (12 sts)
Rnd 2 (dc1, dc2 into next st) 6 times (18)
Rnd 3 (dc2, dc2 into next st) 6 times (24)
Rnd 4 (dc3, dc2 into next st) 6 times (30)
Rnd 5 (dc4, dc2 into next st) 6 times (36)
Rnd 6 (dc5, dc2 into next st) 6 times (42)
Rnds 7–8 dc (2 rnds)
Rnd 9 (dc6, dc2 into next st) 6 times (48)
Rnds 10–14 dc (5 rnds)
Rnd 15 (dc6, dc2tog) 6 times (42)
Rnds 16–18 dc (3 rnds)
Rnd 19 (dc5, dc2tog) 6 times (36)
Rnds 20–22 dc (3 rnds)
Rnd 23 (dc2tog, dc10) 3 times (33)
Rnd 24 dc
Rnd 25 (dc2tog, dc9) 3 times (30)
Rnds 26–30 dc (5 rnds)
Rnd 31 (dc3, dc2tog) 3 times, dc15 (27)
Rnds 32–34 dc (3 rnds)
Rnd 35 dc12, (dc2tog, dc3) 3 times (24)
Rnds 36–38 dc (3 rnds)
Rnd 39 (dc2, dc2tog) 6 times (18)
Rnds 40–42 dc (3 rnds)
Rnd 43 (dc1, dc2tog) 3 times, dc9 (15)
Rnd 44 dc

Rnd 45 (dc2tog) 3 times, dc9 (12)
Rnds 46–50 dc (5 rnds)
Stuff and continue
Rnd 51 dc6, (dc2tog) 3 times (9)
Rnds 52–54 dc (3 rnds)
Rnd 55 dc3, (dc2tog) 3 times (6)
Rnds 56–58 dc (3 rnds)

LINES
Working in Oatmeal
Work lines of SLIP STITCH TRAVERSE onto top section of body in following lengths:
Top 12 sts
Middle 18 sts
Bottom 12 sts

LEAVES
Working in Green
Make STEMS and then work LEAVES around edge of each STEM.

STEM (make three)
Begin by dc6 into ring
Rnds 1–38 dc (38 rnds)
Break yarn.

LEAF
Continues overleaf

MADE IN Oatmeal and Green
YARN QUANTITIES 50g Vegetable, 50g Foliage
TIME TO GROW Moderate
REQUIRES tr, dtr, ttr, qtr, slip stitch traverse

Sl st into position 14 rnds down stem and then
   work along stem towards top as follows:
ch3, tr1, dtr1, ttr2, qtr5, ttr1, dtr2
dc3 in top of STEM and then continue to work
   down other side as follows:
dtr2, ttr1, qtr5, ttr2, dtr1, tr2
Break yarn.

Rejoin at top of starting chain and then work
   around edge as follows:
*ch3, turn and sl st 1, dc1 back down chain, dc1
   along LEAF, rep from * to end
Break yarn.

LEGS (make two)
Working in Green
Begin by dc6 into ring
Rnd 1 (dc2 into next st) 6 times (12)
Rnd 2 (dc1, dc2 into next st) 6 times (18)

Rnd 3 (dc2, dc2 into next st) 6 times (24)
Rnd 4 (dc3, dc2 into next st) 6 times (30)
Rnds 5–7 dc (3 rnds)
Rnd 8 (dc3, dc2tog) 3 times, dc15 (27)
Rnd 9 (dc2, dc2tog) 3 times, dc15 (24)
Rnd 10 (dc2tog) 12 times (12)
Rnds 11–28 dc (18 rnds)

SEWING UP
1. Gather final stitches of BODY to close.
2. Sew in all ends on LEAVES and sew the three
   LEAVES together at bottom.
3. Sew LEAVES into position on top of head.
4. Stuff feet and sew tops of LEGS flat
   perpendicular to foot, then sew into position
   on sides of BODY.
5. Embroider eyes with Black and Cream yarn.

Radish

Radishes grow so quickly that even the most impatient gardener can wait for these peppery roots to be ready to eat. This is a quick, smaller project that will crochet up even before the first spouts peep through the soil.

BODY
The body is worked from the top down.
Working in Magenta
Begin by dc6 into ring
Rnd 1 (dc2 into next st) 6 times (12 sts)
Rnd 2 (dc1, dc2 into next st) 6 times (18)
Rnd 3 (dc2, dc2 into next st) 6 times (24)
Rnd 4 (dc3, dc2 into next st) 6 times (30)
Rnd 5 (dc4, dc2 into next st) 6 times (36)
Rnd 6 dc
Rnd 7 (dc5, dc2 into next st) 6 times (42)
Rnd 8 (dc6, dc2 into next st) 6 times (48)
Rnds 9–16 dc (8 rnds)
Rnd 17 (dc2tog, dc6) 6 times (42)
Rnd 18 (dc2tog, dc5) 6 times (36)
Rnd 19 dc
Rnd 20 (dc2tog, dc4) 6 times (30)
Rnd 21 (dc2tog, dc3) 6 times (24)
Rnd 22 (dc2tog, dc2) 6 times (18)
Change to Cream
Rnd 23 (dc2tog) 9 times (9)
Stuff and continue
Rnd 24 dc
Rnd 25 dc2tog, dc7 (8)
Rnd 26 (dc2tog, dc2) twice (6)
Rnd 27 (dc2tog, dc1) twice (4)
Rnd 28 dc
Ch8, turn and work back down chain as follows:
sl st4, dc4, sl st into body

LEAVES
Working in Lime
Make STEMS and then work LEAVES around edge of each STEM.

STEM (make three)
Begin by dc6 into ring
Rnds 1–38 dc (38 rnds)
Break yarn.

LEAVES
Sl st into position 13 rnds from top of STEM and then work up towards top as follows:
ch2, tr1, dtr2, ttr8, dtr1
tr2 into top of stem and then continue to work down other side as follows:
dtr1, ttr8, dtr2, tr1, dc1
Break yarn.

LEGS (make two)
Working in Lime
Begin by dc6 into ring
Rnd 1 (dc2 into next st) 6 times (12)
Rnd 2 (dc1, dc2 into next st) 6 times (18)
Rnds 3–5 dc (3 rnds)
Rnd 6 (dc2tog) 6 times, dc6 (12)
Rnd 7 (dc2tog) 3 times, dc6 (9)
Rnds 8–18 dc (11 rnds)

Continues overleaf

MADE IN Magenta, Cream and Lime
YARN QUANTITIES 25g Vegetable, 25g Contrast, 25g Foliage
TIME TO GROW Quick
REQUIRES tr, dtr, ttr, colour change

SEWING UP

1. Sew in all ends on LEAVES and sew the three LEAVES together at bottom.
2. Sew LEAVES into position on top of BODY.
3. Stuff feet and sew tops of LEGS flat perpendicular to foot and sew into position on bottom of BODY.
4. Embroider eyes with Black and Cream yarn, and mouth with Black yarn.

Cabbage

A nutritional powerhouse, the red cabbage is another vegetable that has been used to dye textiles for centuries, creating a natural 'blue' hue. Boil up some chopped cabbage until there's no colour left in the vegetable, drain the water and allow it to cool before using salt to fix the colour onto your fabric.

BACK

Working in Lime
Begin by dc6 into ring
Rnd 1 (dc2 into next st) 6 times (12 sts)
Rnd 2 (dc1, dc2 into next st) 6 times (18)
Rnd 3 (dc2, dc2 into next st) 6 times (24)
Rnd 4 (dc3, dc2 into next st) 6 times (30)
Rnd 5 (dc4, dc2 into next st) 6 times (36)
Rnd 6 (dc5, dc2 into next st) 6 times (42)
Rnd 7 (dc6, dc2 into next st) 6 times (48)
Rnd 8 (dc7, dc2 into next st) 6 times (54)
Rnd 9 (dc8, dc2 into next st) 6 times (60)
Rnd 10 (dc9, dc2 into next st) 6 times (66)
Rnd 11 (dc10, dc2 into next st) 6 times (72)
Rnd 12 dc
Rnd 13 (dc11, dc2 into next st) 6 times (78)
Rnd 14 dc
Rnd 15 (dc12, dc2 into next st) 6 times (84)
Rnd 16 dc
Rnd 17 (dc13, dc2 into next st) 6 times (90)
Rnd 18 dc
Rnd 19 (dc14, dc2 into next st) 6 times (96)
Rnd 20 dc
Rnd 21 (dc15, dc2 into next st) 6 times (102)
Rnds 22–23 dc (2 rnds)

FRONT

Working in Lime
Begin by dc6 into ring

Rnd 1 (dc2 into next st) 6 times (12)
Rnd 2 (dc1, dc2 into next st) 6 times (18)
Rnd 3 (dc2, dc2 into next st) 6 times (24)
Rnd 4 (dc3, dc2 into next st) 6 times (30)
Rnd 5 (dc4, dc2 into next st) 6 times (36)
Rnd 6 (dc5, dc2 into next st) 6 times (42)
Rnd 7 (dc6, dc2 into next st) 6 times (48)
Rnd 8 (dc7, dc2 into next st) 6 times (54)
Rnd 9 (dc8, dc2 into next st) 6 times (60)
Rnd 10 (dc9, dc2 into next st) 6 times (66)
Rnd 11 (dc10, dc2 into next st) 6 times (72)
Rnd 12 (dc11, dc2 into next st) 6 times (78)
Rnd 13 (dc12, dc2 into next st) 6 times (84)
Rnd 14 (dc13, dc2 into next st) 6 times (90)
Rnd 15 (dc14, dc2 into next st) 6 times (96)
Rnd 16 (dc15, dc2 into next st) 6 times (102)

CORE

Working in Cream
Ch16, turn and work back down chain as
    follows:
*dc3, htr3, tr3, dtr3, ttr3
Break yarn, rejoin at top and repeat from *
    down other side of chain.

Ch13, turn and work back down chain as
    follows:
sl st3, dc3, htr3, tr3
Continues overleaf

MADE IN Cream and Lime and (overleaf in Magenta)
YARN QUANTITIES 50g Leaves, 25g Core
TIME TO GROW Slow
REQUIRES htr, tr, dtr, ttr, dc traverse

Miss 2 sts, dc2 along base

Ch10, turn and work back down chain as
  follows:
sl st3, dc3, htr3
Miss 2 sts, dc2 along base

Ch7, turn and work back down chain as follows:
sl st2, dc2, htr2
Miss 2 sts, dc2 along base

Ch3, turn and work back down chain as follows:
sl st1, dc1
Miss 2 sts, dc1 along base

Dc1 into top of base and then work lengths in
  reverse down other side.

LEGS (make two)

Working in Cream
Follow instructions for Turnip on page 68.

SEWING UP

1. Using Cream attach FRONT and BACK
   pieces together with SL ST TO JOIN TWO
   PIECES TOGETHER (see below) around
   edge from the inside out. Stuff before
   fully closed.
2. Stuff feet, sew top of LEGS flat and sew into
   position on joining edge at bottom.
3. Sew CORE into position on FRONT by
   sewing around edge.
4. Embroider eyes with Black and Cream yarn.

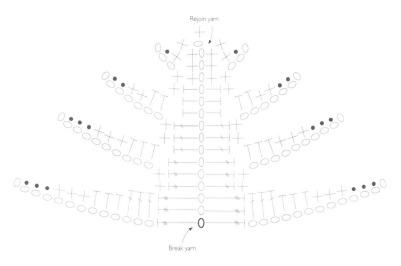

SL ST TO JOIN TWO PIECES TOGETHER

1   With yarn on bottom of
    both pieces of crochet,
    insert hook from top to
    bottom through both
    layers of fabric.

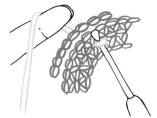

2   Yarn over and bring
    through both layers
    of fabric.

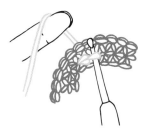

3   Pull through final loop.

Turnip

The turnip's bright purple top is created by the sun falling on the part of the vegetable that peeps up above the soil. Reminiscent of a superhero in a mask, this cute character might persuade a fussy eater to try something new.

BODY
The body is worked from the bottom up.
Working in Cream
Begin by dc6 into ring
Rnd 1 (dc2 into next st) 6 times (12 sts)
Rnd 2 (dc1, dc2 into next st) 6 times (18)
Rnd 3 (dc2, dc2 into next st) 6 times (24)
Rnd 4 (dc3, dc2 into next st) 6 times (30)
Rnd 5 (dc4, dc2 into next st) 6 times (36)
Rnd 6 dc
Rnd 7 (dc5, dc2 into next st) 6 times (42)
Rnds 8–9 dc (2 rnds)
Rnd 10 (dc6, dc2 into next st) 6 times (48)
Rnds 11–12 dc (2 rnds)
Change to Amethyst
Rnd 13 (dc7, dc2 into next st) 6 times (54)
Rnds 14–18 dc (5 rnds)
Rnd 19 (dc7, dc2tog) 6 times (48)
Rnds 20–21 dc (2 rnds)
Rnd 22 (dc2tog, dc6) 6 times (42)
Rnd 23 dc
Rnd 24 (dc2tog, dc5) 6 times (36)
Rnd 25 dc
Rnd 26 (dc2tog, dc4) 6 times (30)
Rnd 27 (dc2tog, dc3) 6 times (24)
Rnd 28 (dc2tog, dc2) 6 times (18)
Rnd 29 (dc2tog) 9 times (9)
Stuff and continue
Rnd 30 (dc2tog, dc1) 3 times (6)
Rnd 31 dc

LEAVES
Working in Green
Make STEMS and then work LEAVES around edge of each STEM.

STEM (make three)
Begin by dc6 into ring
Rnds 1–28 dc (28 rnds)
Break yarn.

LEAVES
Sl st into position 20 rnds down from top of STEM and work tr2 into every stitch along STEM towards top, then down opposite side.
Break yarn.

LEGS (make two)
Working in Green
Begin by dc6 into ring
Rnd 1 (dc2 into next st) 6 times (12)
Rnd 2 (dc1, dc2 into next st) 6 times (18)
Rnd 3 (dc2, dc2 into next st) 6 times (24)
Rnd 4 (dc3, dc2 into next st) 6 times (30)
Rnds 5–7 dc (3 rnds)
Rnd 8 (dc3, dc2tog) 3 times, dc15 (27)
Rnd 9 (dc2, dc2tog) 3 times, dc15 (24)
Rnd 10 (dc2tog) 12 times (12)
Rnds 11–18 dc (8 rnds)
Continues overleaf

MADE IN Amethyst, Cream and Green
YARN QUANTITIES 25g Vegetable, 25g Contrast, 50g Foliage
TIME TO GROW Quick
REQUIRES tr, colour change

SEWING UP

1. Gather final stitches of BODY to close. Sew directly through central ring, pull tight and fasten off at the bottom to invert the top.
2. Sew in all ends on LEAVES and sew three LEAVES together at bottom.
3. Sew LEAVES into position on top of BODY.
4. Stuff feet and sew tops of LEGS flat perpendicular to foot, then sew into position on bottom of BODY.
5. Embroider eyes with Black and Cream yarn.

Avocado

A fashionable fruit for the last decade, and a very fun make, with its removable seed in the centre. Although not one for the garden, it's an easy plant to grow on your windowsill in a glass of water, with the seed balanced on a few toothpicks – once you've enjoyed a good breakfast of avocado on toast.

FLESH

Working in Lime
Begin by dc6 into ring
Rnd 1 (dc2 into next st) 6 times (12 sts)
Rnd 2 (dc1, dc2 into next st) 6 times (18)
Rnd 3 (dc2, dc2 into next st) 6 times (24)
Rnd 4 dc
Rnd 5 (dc3, dc2 into next st) 6 times (30)
Rnds 6–9 dc (4 rnds)
Working into back loop only
Rnd 10 (dc2, dc2 into next st) 10 times (40)
Continue working through whole stitch
Rnd 11 dc3, (dc2 into next st) 4 times, dc3, (dc2 into next st, dc2) 10 times (54)
Rnd 12 dc
Rnd 13 dc6, (dc2 into next st) twice, dc6, (dc2 into next st, dc7) 4 times, dc2 into next st, dc6, dc2 into next st (62)
Rnd 14 dc8, (dc2 into next st) twice, dc10, (dc2 into next st, dc7) 5 times, dc2 into next st, dc1 (70)
Rnd 15 dc9, (dc2 into next st) twice, dc24, (dc2 into next st, dc3) 5 times, dc2 into next st, dc14 (78)
Rnd 16 dc10, (dc2 into next st) twice and place centraliser between the two increases, dc24, (dc2 into next st, dc4) 5 times, dc2 into next st, dc16 (86)
Rnd 17 dc

SKIN

Working in Green
Begin by dc6 into ring
Rnd 1 (dc2 into next st) 6 times (12)
Rnd 2 (dc1, dc2 into next st) 6 times (18)
Rnd 3 (dc2, dc2 into next st) 6 times (24)
Rnd 4 dc
Rnd 5 (dc3, dc2 into next st) 6 times (30)
Rnd 6 (dc4, dc2 into next st) 6 times (36)
Rnd 7 (dc8, dc2 into next st) 4 times (40)
Rnd 8 dc3, (dc2 into next st) 4 times, dc3, (dc2 into next st, dc2) 10 times (54)
Rnd 9 dc6, (dc2 into next st) twice, dc6, (dc2 into next st, dc7) 4 times, dc2 into next st, dc6, dc2 into next st (62)
Rnd 10 dc
Rnd 11 dc8, (dc2 into next st) twice, dc10, (dc2 into next st, dc7) 5 times, dc2 into next st, dc1 (70)
Rnd 12 dc
Rnd 13 dc9, (dc2 into next st) twice, dc24, (dc2 into next st, dc3) 5 times, dc2 into next st, dc14 (78)
Rnd 14 dc
Rnd 15 dc10, (dc2 into next st) twice and place centraliser between the two increases, dc24, (dc2 into next st, dc4) 5 times, dc2 into next st, dc16 (86)
Continues overleaf

MADE IN Green, Lime and Chestnut
YARN QUANTITIES 50g Skin, 25g Flesh, 25g Seed
TIME TO GROW Slow
REQUIRES Back loop

Rnds 16–19 dc (4 rnds)

SEED
Working in Chestnut
Begin by dc6 into ring
Rnd 1 (dc2 into next st) 6 times (12)
Rnd 2 (dc1, dc2 into next st) 6 times (18)
Rnd 3 (dc2, dc2 into next st) 6 times (24)
Rnd 4 dc
Rnd 5 (dc3, dc2 into next st) 6 times (30)
Rnds 6–10 dc (5 rnds)
Rnd 11 (dc3, dc2tog) 6 times (24)
Rnd 12 dc
Rnd 13 (dc2, dc2tog) 6 times (18)
Rnd 14 (dc1, dc2tog) 6 times (12)
Rnd 15 (dc2tog) 6 times (6)

LEGS (make two)
Working in Green
Begin by dc6 into ring
Rnd 1 (dc2 into next st) 6 times (12)
Rnd 2 (dc1, dc2 into next st) 6 times (18)
Rnd 3 (dc2, dc2 into next st) 6 times (24)
Rnd 4 (dc3, dc2 into next st) 6 times (30)
Rnds 5–7 dc (3 rnds)
Rnd 8 (dc3, dc2tog) 3 times, dc15 (27)
Rnd 9 (dc2, dc2tog) 3 times, dc15 (24)
Rnd 10 (dc2tog) 12 times (12)
Rnds 11–23 dc (13 rnds)

ARMS (make two)
Working in Green
Begin by dc6 into ring
Rnd 1 (dc2 into next st) 6 times (12)
Rnd 2 (dc1, dc2 into next st) 6 times (18)
Rnd 3 (dc2, dc2 into next st) 6 times (24)
Rnds 4–8 dc (5 rnds)
Rnd 9 dc6, (dc1, dc2tog) 6 times (18)
Rnd 10 dc6, (dc2tog) 6 times (12)
Rnds 11–22 dc (12 rnds)

SEWING UP
1. Line up centraliser markers on SKIN and
   FLESH, ensuring that right sides are facing
   outwards. Attach with a round of dc from
   the outside in using Green. Stuff before
   fully closed.
2. Stuff feet and sew top of LEGS flat, then sew
   into position onto joining edge at bottom
   of SKIN.
3. Stuff hands and sew tops of ARMS flat
   perpendicular to hand, then sew into
   position on sides of BODY.
4. Stuff SEED and gather stitches to close.
5. Embroider eyes with Black and Cream yarn.

Baby Cucumber

This is a vegetable with many names! Enjoy fresh from the plant as a cucumber, or ferment it and it becomes a pickle, gherkin, dill or cornichon.

MLB Make Large Bobble (through on fifth repeat)
(yarn over hook, insert hook into stitch, yarn over and bring through, yarn over and bring through first 2 loops) 4 times, yarn over hook, insert hook into stitch, yarn over and bring through, yarn over and bring through all loops on hook.

BODY

The body is worked from the bottom up.
Working in Green
Begin by dc6 into ring
Rnd 1 (dc2 into next st) 6 times (12 sts)
Rnd 2 (MLB, dc2 into next st, dc1, dc2 into next st) 3 times (18)
Rnd 3 dc
Rnd 4 (dc2, dc2 into next st) 6 times (24)
Rnd 5 (MLB, dc2, dc2 into next st) 6 times (30)
Rnds 6–7 dc (2 rnds)
Rnd 8 (MLB, dc4) 6 times
Rnds 9–10 dc (2 rnds)
Rnd 11 (MLB, dc4) 6 times
Rnds 12–13 dc (2 rnds)
Rnd 14 (MLB, dc4) 6 times
Rnd 15 dc
Rnd 16 (dc2tog, dc3) 3 times, (dc2 into next, dc4) 3 times (30)
Rnd 17 (MLB, dc3) twice, MLB, dc4, MLB, (dc5, MLB) twice, dc4
Rnds 18–19 dc (2 rnds)

Rnd 20 (MLB, dc4) 6 times
Rnds 21–22 dc (2 rnds)
Rnd 23 (MLB, dc4) 6 times
Rnds 24–25 dc (2 rnds)
Rnd 26 (MLB, dc4) 6 times
Rnd 27 dc
Rnd 28 (dc3, dc2tog) 6 times (24)
Rnd 29 (MLB, dc1, dc2tog, dc2, dc2tog) 3 times (18)
Rnd 30 dc
Rnd 31 (dc2tog) 9 times (9)
Rnd 32 (dc1, dc2tog) 3 times (6)

CALYX

Working in Sage
Begin by dc5 into ring
*ch3, turn and sl st1, dc1 back down chain, dc1 along base
Repeat from * four more times.
Break yarn.

LEGS (make two)

Working in Sage
Begin by dc6 into ring
Rnd 1 (dc2 into next st) 6 times (12)
Rnd 2 (dc1, dc2 into next st) 6 times (18)
Rnds 3–5 dc (3 rnds)
Rnd 6 (dc2tog) 6 times, dc6 (12)
Rnd 7 (dc2tog) 3 times, dc6 (9)
Rnds 8–15 dc (8 rnds)
Continues overleaf

MADE IN Green and Sage (overleaf in Kale)
YARN QUANTITIES 25g Fruit, 25g Foliage
TIME TO GROW Quick
REQUIRES Bobbles

SEWING UP

1. Stuff BODY and gather final stitches to close.
2. Sew CALYX into position on top of body.
3. Working in Sage, sl st into position at centre of CALYX, ch4, turn and sl st 3 back down chain to create a stalk.
4. Stuff feet and sew tops of LEGS flat perpendicular to foot, then sew into position on bottom of body.
5. Embroider eyes with Black and Cream yarn, and mouth with Black yarn.

Asparagus

Sow some asparagus seeds and you'll need to wait three years for the plants to mature before you can cook them for dinner. Just like the real thing, this project is easy to make but it will require a little more patience than others.

BODY

The body is worked from the bottom up.
Working in Lime
Ch30 and sl st to join into a circle
Rnds 1–3 dc (3 rnds)
Rnd 4 (dc3, dc2tog) 6 times (24 sts)
Rnds 5–24 dc (20 rnds)
Rnd 25 (dc2tog, dc6) 3 times (21)
Rnds 26–33 dc (8 rnds)
Rnd 34 (dc2, dc2 into next st) 7 times (28)
Rnd 35 (dc13, dc2 into next st) twice (30)
Change to Green
Rnd 36 (dc4, dc2 into next st) 6 times (36)
Rnds 37–48 dc (12 rnds)
Rnd 49 (dc2tog, dc4) 6 times (30)
Rnd 50 dc
Rnd 51 (dc2tog, dc3) 6 times (24)
Rnd 52 dc
Rnd 53 (dc2tog, dc2) 6 times (18)
Rnd 54 dc
Rnd 55 (dc2tog, dc1) 6 times (12)
Rnd 56 dc
Rnd 57 (dc2tog, dc2) 3 times (9)

BASE

Working in Lime
Begin by dc6 into ring
Rnd 1 (dc2 into next st) 6 times (12)
Rnd 2 (dc1, dc2 into next st) 6 times (18)
Rnd 3 (dc2, dc2 into next st) 6 times (24)

Rnd 4 (dc3, dc2 into next st) 6 times (30)

SCALE LEAVES (make 15)

Working in Lime
Begin by dc6 into ring
Rnd 1 (htr2 into next st) 6 times (12)
Rnds 2–3 tr (2 rnds)
Rnd 4 (tr1, tr2tog) 4 times (8)
Rnd 5 (dc2tog) 4 times (4)
Break yarn and gather sts to close top.

Working in Green
Fold flat and dc around edge of each
    SPEAR as follows:
sl st into position at bottom corner, dc2 into
    first st, dc7 along edge, dc2 into top, dc7
    down edge, dc2 into next st
Break yarn.

Working in Green
Make a ring of five SPEARS by dc5 along
    wide end with ch1 between SPEARS to join
    together (30)
Make a second ring of five SPEARS by dc5
    along the wide end with ch2 between
    spears to join together (35)
Make a third ring of five SPEARS the same as
    the first (30)

Continues overleaf

MADE IN Lime and Green
YARN QUANTITIES 75g Main, 25g Contrast
TIME TO GROW Slow
REQUIRES htr, tr, colour change, ring of leaves

LEGS (make two)

Working in Lime
Begin by dc6 into ring
Rnd 1 (dc2 into next st) 6 times (12)
Rnd 2 (dc1, dc2 into next st) 6 times (18)
Rnd 3 (dc2, dc2 into next st) 6 times (24)
Rnd 4 (dc3, dc2 into next st) 6 times (30)
Rnds 5–7 dc (3 rnds)
Rnd 8 (dc3, dc2tog) 3 times, dc15 (27)
Rnd 9 (dc2, dc2tog) 3 times, dc15 (24)
Rnd 10 (dc2tog) 12 times (12)
Rnds 11–18 dc (8 rnds)

ARMS (make two)

Working in Lime
Begin by dc6 into ring
Rnd 1 (dc2 into next st) 6 times (12)
Rnd 2 (dc1, dc2 into next st) 6 times (18)
Rnd 3 (dc2, dc2 into next st) 6 times (24)
Rnds 4–8 dc (5 rnds)
Rnd 9 dc6, (dc1, dc2tog) 6 times (18)
Rnd 10 dc6, (dc2tog) 6 times (12)
Rnds 11–22 dc (12 rnds)

SEWING UP

1. Stuff BODY and join BASE to BODY with a round of dc from the bottom up.
2. Ensuring dc stitches are right-side facing, place one of the 30-st rings of SPEARS around colour change round of BODY and sew bottom into position around colour change round.
3. Place 35-st ring of SPEARS around widest part of top and sew bottom into position, ensuring SPEARS are placed between those on ring below.
4. Place other 30-st ring of SPEARS around top and sew bottom into position, ensuring SPEARS are placed between those on ring below.
5. Sew tips of SPEARS on bottom two rings to gap above to secure.
6. Stuff and sew top of LEGS flat and sew into position on joining edge of BASE.
7. Stuff hands and sew tops of ARMS flat perpendicular to hand, then sew into position on sides of BODY.
8. Embroider eyes with Black and Cream yarn.

Onion

Whether red, yellow or white, the humble onion always delivers on flavour, transforming any dish into something delicious. Onions are known for making us cry, but this cuddly character is more likely to prompt a smile than a tear.

BODY

The body is worked from the bottom up.
Working in Camel
Begin by dc6 into ring
Rnd 1 (dc2 into next st) 6 times (12 sts)
Rnd 2 (dc1, dc2 into next st) 6 times (18)
Rnd 3 (dc2, dc2 into next st) 6 times (24)
Rnd 4 (dc3, dc2 into next st) 6 times (30)
Working into back loop only
Rnd 5 dc
Continue working through whole stitch
Rnd 6 (dc4, dc2 into next st) 6 times (36)
Rnd 7 (dc5, dc2 into next st) 6 times (42)
Rnd 8 (dc6, dc2 into next st) 6 times (48)
Rnd 9 (dc7, dc2 into next st) 6 times (54)
Rnd 10 dc
Rnd 11 (dc8, dc2 into next st) 6 times (60)
Rnd 12 dc
Rnd 13 (dc9, dc2 into next st) 6 times (66)
Rnd 14 (dc10, dc2 into next st) 6 times (72)
Rnds 15–24 dc (10 rnds)
Rnd 25 (dc10, dc2tog) 6 times (66)
Rnd 26 (dc9, dc2tog) 6 times (60)
Rnd 27 dc
Rnd 28 (dc8, dc2tog) 6 times (54)
Rnd 29 dc
Rnd 30 (dc7, dc2tog) 6 times (48)
Rnd 31 dc
Rnd 32 (dc6, dc2tog) 6 times (42)
Rnd 33 dc

Rnd 34 (dc5, dc2tog) 6 times (36)
Rnd 35 dc
Rnd 36 (dc4, dc2tog) 6 times (30)
Rnd 37 dc
Rnd 38 (dc3, dc2tog) 6 times (24)
Rnd 39 (dc2, dc2tog) 6 times (18)
Rnds 40–41 dc (2 rnds)
Rnd 42 (dc1, htr1, tr1, htr1, dc1, sl st1) 3 times
Break yarn and leave long end for sewing up.
Stuff body and leave top open. Don't sew end in yet.

ROOTS

Working in Camel
Sl st into position on bottom of body one round in from back loop round.
*Ch6, turn and work back down chain as follows:
sl st2, dc2 into next st, dc2
SLIP STITCH TRAVERSE 2 sts along round and repeat from * eight more times

SHOOTS

SHORT
Working in Cream
Begin by dc6 into ring
Rnd 1 (dc2 into next st) 6 times (12)
Rnd 2 (dc3, dc2 into next st) 3 times (15)
Rnds 3–4 dc (2 rnds)
Continues overleaf

MADE IN Camel, Cream and Chive (overleaf in Beetroot, Cream and Green)
YARN QUANTITIES 50g Bulb, 25g Shoots, 25g Leaves
TIME TO GROW Moderate
REQUIRES htr, tr, back loop, colour change

Change to Chive
Rnds 5–11 dc (7 rnds)
Rnd 12 dc2tog, dc13 (14)
Rnd 13 dc2tog, dc12 (13)
Rnd 14 dc2tog, dc11 (12)
Rnd 15 dc2tog, dc10 (11)
Rnd 16 dc2tog, dc9 (10)
Rnd 17 dc2tog, dc8 (9)
Rnd 18 dc2tog, dc7 (8)
Rnd 19 dc2tog, dc6 (7)

MEDIUM
Working in Cream
Begin by dc6 into ring
Rnd 1 (dc2 into next st) 6 times (12)
Rnd 2 (dc3, dc2 into next st) 3 times (15)
Rnds 3–7 dc (5 rnds)
Change to Chive
Rnds 8–14 dc (7 rnds)
Rnd 15 dc2tog, dc13 (14)
Rnd 16 dc2tog, dc12 (13)
Rnd 17 dc2tog, dc11 (12)
Rnd 18 dc2tog, dc10 (11)
Rnd 19 dc2tog, dc9 (10)
Rnd 20 dc2tog, dc8 (9)
Rnd 21 dc2tog, dc7 (8)
Rnd 22 dc2tog, dc6 (7)

LONG
Working in Cream
Begin by dc6 into ring
Rnd 1 (dc2 into next st) 6 times (12)
Rnd 2 (dc3, dc2 into next st) 3 times (15)

Rnds 3–10 dc (8 rnds)
Change to Chive
Rnds 11–17 dc (7 rnds)
Rnd 18 dc2tog, dc13 (14)
Rnd 19 dc2tog, dc12 (13)
Rnd 20 dc2tog, dc11 (12)
Rnd 21 dc2tog, dc10 (11)
Rnd 22 dc2tog, dc9 (10)
Rnd 23 dc2tog, dc8 (9)
Rnd 24 dc2tog, dc7 (8)
Rnd 25 dc2tog, dc6 (7)

LEGS (make two)
Working in Cream
Begin by dc6 into ring
Rnd 1 (dc2 into next st) 6 times (12)
Rnd 2 (dc1, dc2 into next st) 6 times (18)
Rnd 3 (dc2, dc2 into next st) 6 times (24)
Rnd 4 (dc3, dc2 into next st) 6 times (30)
Rnds 5–7 dc (3 rnds)
Rnd 8 (dc3, dc2tog) 3 times, dc15 (27)
Rnd 9 (dc2, dc2tog) 3 times, dc15 (24)
Rnd 10 (dc2tog) 12 times (12)
Rnds 11–23 dc (13 rnds)

SEWING UP
1. Stuff SHOOTS and gather stitches to close.
2. Insert SHOOTS into open top of BODY.
   Sew into place using yarn end from BODY.
4. Stuff feet and sew top of LEGS flat, then sew
   into position on bottom of BODY.
5. Embroider eyes with Black and Cream yarn.

Broad Bean

Broad beans, or fava beans, are easy to grow, and low maintenance; they like to be planted in a sheltered, sunny spot with well-drained soil. Children will enjoy putting these cheery characters to sleep in their pod-bed after a day of playing in the garden.

NOTE
Three beans will fit perfectly into your pod but the amount of yarn specified is enough to make up to four beans.

BEANS
Working in Sage
Ch4 and work around the chain
Rnd 1 dc2, dc2 into next st along one side of chain, dc2, dc2 into next st along other side of chain (8)
Rnd 2 (dc2, dc2 into next st, dc2 into next st) twice (12)
Rnd 3 dc3, (dc2 into next st) 3 times, dc3, (dc2 into next st) 3 times (18)
Rnd 4 (dc2, dc2 into next st) 6 times (24)
Rnd 5 (dc3, dc2 into next st) 6 times (30)
Rnds 6–10 dc (5 rnds)
Rnd 11 (dc1, dc2tog) 5 times, dc15 (25)
Rnds 12–13 dc (2 rnds)
Rnd 14 (dc1, dc2 into next st) 5 times, dc15 (30)
Rnds 15–19 dc (5 rnds)
Rnd 20 (dc3, dc2tog) 6 times (24)
Rnd 21 (dc2, dc2tog) 6 times (18)
Rnd 22 dc3, (dc2tog) 3 times, dc3, (dc2tog) 3 times (12)
Rnd 23 dc3, (dc2tog) twice, dc3, dc2tog (9)

POD
Working in Green
Ch41 and work around the chain
Rnd 1 dc39, dc2 into next st along one side of chain, dc39, dc2 into next st along other side of chain (82)
Rnd 2 dc2 into next st, dc2, dc2 into next st, dc33, dc2 into next st, dc2, (dc2 into next st) twice, dc2, dc2 into next st, dc33, dc2 into next st, dc2, dc2 into next (90)
Rnd 3 (dc8, dc2 into next st) 10 times (100)
Rnd 4 (dc2 into next st, dc49) twice (102)
Rnds 5–10 dc (6 rnds)
Rnd 11 dc2tog, dc2, dc2tog, dc45, dc2tog, dc2, dc2tog, dc45 (98)
Rnd 12 (dc2tog) twice, dc45, (dc2tog) twice, dc45 (94)
Rnd 13 (dc2tog) twice, dc43, (dc2tog) twice, dc43 (90)
Rnd 14 dc
Rnd 15 (dc2tog, dc7) 10 times (80)
Rnd 16 (dc2tog, dc6) 10 times (70)

LEGS (make two)
Working in Green
Begin by dc6 into ring
Rnd 1 (dc2 into next st) 6 times (12)
Continues overleaf

MADE IN Sage and Green
YARN QUANTITIES 50g Bean, 50g Foliage
TIME TO GROW Moderate
REQUIRES Working around a chain

Rnd 2 (dc1, dc2 into next st) 6 times (18)
Rnd 3 (dc2, dc2 into next st) 6 times (24)
Rnd 4 (dc3, dc2 into next st) 6 times (30)
Rnds 5–7 dc (3 rnds)
Rnd 8 (dc3, dc2tog) 3 times, dc15 (27)
Rnd 9 (dc2, dc2tog) 3 times, dc15 (24)
Rnd 10 (dc2tog) 12 times (12)
Rnds 11–18 dc (8 rnds)

ARMS (make two)
Working in Green
Begin by dc6 into ring
Rnd 1 (dc2 into next st) 6 times (12)
Rnd 2 (dc1, dc2 into next st) 6 times (18)
Rnd 3 (dc2, dc2 into next st) 6 times (24)
Rnds 4–8 dc (5 rnds)

Rnd 9 dc6, (dc1, dc2tog) 6 times (18)
Rnd 10 dc6, (dc2tog) 6 times (12)
Rnds 11–22 dc (12 rnds)

SEWING UP
1. Stuff beans and gather final stitches to close.
2. Stuff feet and sew tops of legs flat perpendicular to foot, then sew into position on bottom of pod.
3. Stuff hands and sew tops of arms flat perpendicular to hand, then sew into position on sides of pod.
4. Embroider eyes onto beans with Black and Cream yarn, and add facial expressions as desired with Black yarn.

Artichoke

An artichoke is an unbloomed flower, and is actually a variety of thistle. Always cooked before eating, you remove and eat the petals separately to the 'choke' at the centre – the reverse of how you'll crochet and construct this project.

BODY

The body is worked from the bottom up.
Working in Lime
Begin by dc6 into ring
Rnd 1 (dc2 into next st) 6 times (12 sts)
Rnd 2 (dc1, dc2 into next st) 6 times (18)
Rnd 3 (dc2, dc2 into next st) 6 times (24)
Rnd 4 (dc3, dc2 into next st) 6 times (30)
Rnd 5 (dc4, dc2 into next st) 6 times (36)
Rnd 6 (dc5, dc2 into next st) 6 times (42)
Rnd 7 (dc6, dc2 into next st) 6 times (48)
Rnd 8 dc
Rnd 9 (dc7, dc2 into next st) 6 times (54)
Rnd 10 dc
Rnd 11 (dc8, dc2 into next st) 6 times (60)
Rnds 12–21 dc (10 rnds)
Rnd 22 (dc4, dc2tog) 10 times (50)
Rnd 23 (dc3, dc2tog) 10 times (40)
Rnd 24 (dc2, dc2tog) 10 times (30)
Rnd 25 dc
Rnd 26 (dc8, dc2tog) 3 times (27)
Rnd 27 (dc7, dc2tog) 3 times (24)
Rnd 28 (dc2, dc2tog) 6 times (18)
Rnd 29 dc
Rnd 30 (dc2tog) 9 times (9)
Stuff and continue
Rnds 31–32 dc (2 rnds)
Rnd 33 (dc1, dc2tog) 3 times (6)
Rnd 34 dc
Rnd 35 (dc1, dc2tog) twice (4)

PETALS (make 14)

Working in Lime
Begin by dc6 into ring
Rnd 1 (dc2 into next st) 6 times (12)
Rnd 2 (dc1, dc2 into next st) 6 times (18)
Rnd 3 (dc2, dc2 into next st) 6 times (24)
Rnd 4 (dc3, dc2 into next st) 6 times (30)
Rnds 5–9 dc (5 rnds)
Rnd 10 (dc3, dc2tog) 6 times (24)
Rnd 11 dc
Rnd 12 (dc2, dc2tog) 6 times (18)
Rnd 13 dc
Rnd 14 (dc4, dc2tog) 3 times (15)
Rnd 15 dc
Rnd 16 (dc3, dc2tog) 3 times (12)
Rnd 17 (dc2, dc2tog) 3 times (9)
Break yarn and gather sts to close.

Working in Lime
Make a ring of five overlapping petals by dc5 along wide end of each to join together (25)
Make another ring of five petals by dc8 along each with ch2 between petals to join together (50)

LEGS (make two)

Working in Green
Begin by dc6 into ring
Continues overleaf

MADE IN Lime and Green
YARN QUANTITIES 125g Vegetable, 25g Legs
TIME TO GROW Slow
REQUIRES Ring of leaves

Rnd 1 (dc2 into next st) 6 times (12)
Rnd 2 (dc1, dc2 into next st) 6 times (18)
Rnd 3 (dc2, dc2 into next st) 6 times (24)
Rnd 4 (dc3, dc2 into next st) 6 times (30)
Rnds 5–7 dc (3 rnds)
Rnd 8 (dc3, dc2tog) 3 times, dc15 (27)
Rnd 9 (dc2, dc2tog) 3 times, dc15 (24)
Rnd 10 (dc2tog) 12 times (12)
Rnds 11–23 dc (13 rnds)

SEWING UP

1. Gather final stitches of BODY to close.
2. Place 25-st ring of PETALS around bottom of BODY and sew into position.
3. Place 50-st ring of PETALS around widest point of BODY and sew into position.
4. Sew remaining four PETALS into position around top of BODY.
5. Stuff feet and sew top of LEGS flat, then sew into position on bottom of BODY.
6. Embroider eyes with Black and Cream yarn.

Aubergine

The aubergine is part of the tomato and potato family, which are all nightshades, and so this character is in fact botanically a berry and not a vegetable. The plant flowers with stunning violet and yellow flowers, from which these tasty, typically dark purple fruits develop.

BODY

The body is worked from the bottom up.
Working in Cocoa
Begin by dc6 into ring
Rnd 1 (dc2 into next st) 6 times (12)
Rnd 2 (dc1, dc2 into next st) 6 times (18)
Rnd 3 (dc2, dc2 into next st) 6 times (24)
Rnd 4 (dc3, dc2 into next st) 6 times (30)
Rnd 5 (dc4, dc2 into next st) 6 times (36)
Rnd 6 (dc5, dc2 into next st) 6 times (42)
Rnd 7 (dc6, dc2 into next st) 6 times (48)
Rnd 8 (dc7, dc2 into next st) 6 times (54)
Rnd 9 (dc8, dc2 into next st) 6 times (60)
Rnds 10–33 dc (24 rnds)
Rnd 34 (dc2tog, dc8) 6 times (54)
Rnd 35 dc
Rnd 36 (dc2tog, dc7) 6 times (48)
Rnds 37–39 dc (3 rnds)
Rnd 40 (dc2tog, dc6) 6 times (42)
Rnds 41–45 dc (5 rnds)
Rnd 46 (dc2tog, dc5) 6 times (36)
Rnd 47 dc
Rnd 48 (dc2tog, dc4) 6 times (30)
Rnd 49 (dc2tog, dc3) 6 times (24)
Rnd 50 (dc2tog, dc2) 6 times (18)
Rnd 51 (dc2tog, dc1) 6 times (12)
Rnd 52 (dc2tog, dc2) 3 times (9)

STALK

Working in Lime
Begin by dc6 into ring
Rnd 1 (dc1, dc2 into next st) 3 times (9)
Rnds 2–5 dc (4 rnds)
Rnd 6 (dc2, dc2 into next st) 3 times (12)
Rnds 7–10 dc (4 rnds)
Rnd 11 (dc3, dc2 into next st) 3 times (15)
Rnds 12–15 dc (4 rnds)
Rnd 16 (dc2 into next st) 15 times (30)
Rnd 17 (dc4, dc2 into next st) 6 times (36)
Rnd 18 (dc5, dc2 into next st) 6 times (42)
Rnds 19–21 dc (3 rnds)
Rnd 22 dc1, htr1, tr1, dtr1, ttr2, dtr1, tr1, htr1, dc2, htr1, tr2, dtr2, ttr3, dtr2, tr2, htr1, dc1, htr1, tr1, dtr1, ttr3, dtr2, tr1, htr1, dc1, htr1, tr2, htr2, dc1
Rnd 23 dc4, (dc2 into next st) twice, dc10, (dc2 into next st) 3 times, dc9, (dc2 into next st) 3 times, dc11 (50)

LEGS (make two)

Working in Lime
Begin by dc6 into ring
Rnd 1 (dc2 into next st) 6 times (12)
Rnd 2 (dc1, dc2 into next st) 6 times (18)
Rnd 3 (dc2, dc2 into next st) 6 times (24)
Rnd 4 (dc3, dc2 into next st) 6 times (30)
Rnds 5–7 dc (3 rnds)
Continues overleaf

MADE IN Cocoa and Lime
YARN QUANTITIES 50g Vegetable, 50g Foliage
TIME TO GROW Slow
REQUIRES htr, tr, dtr, ttr

Rnd 8 (dc3, dc2tog) 3 times, dc15 (27)
Rnd 9 (dc2, dc2tog) 3 times, dc15 (24)
Rnd 10 (dc2tog) 12 times (12)
Rnds 11–18 dc (8 rnds)

ARMS (make two)

Working in Lime
Begin by dc6 into ring
Rnd 1 (dc2 into next st) 6 times (12)
Rnd 2 (dc1, dc2 into next st) 6 times (18)
Rnd 3 (dc2, dc2 into next st) 6 times (24)
Rnds 4–8 dc (5 rnds)
Rnd 9 dc6, (dc1, dc2tog) 6 times (18)
Rnd 10 dc6, (dc2tog) 6 times (12)
Rnds 11–22 dc (12 rnds)

SEWING UP

1. Stuff BODY and gather final stitches to close.
2. Stuff STALK and sew into position on top of BODY by sewing around last round before the long stitches. (This leaves the edge sitting slightly off the fabric.)
3. Stuff feet and sew top of LEGS flat, then sew into position on bottom of body.
4. Stuff hands and sew tops of ARMS flat perpendicular to hand, then sew into position on sides of BODY.
5. Embroider eyes with Black and Cream yarn.

Peas in a Pod

Although they're perhaps best enjoyed eaten fresh from the pod in late spring, peas can be frozen, canned, dried or mushed, and they've become a staple veg on many of our plates. Ranging from two to twenty peas in a pod, this is one that you'll have lots of fun making over and over again.

PEA (make three)
Working in Lime
Begin by dc6 into ring
Rnd 1 (dc2 into next st) 6 times (12 sts)
Rnd 2 (dc1, dc2 into next st) 6 times (18)
Rnd 3 (dc2, dc2 into next st) 6 times (24)
Rnd 4 dc
Rnd 5 (dc3, dc2 into next st) 6 times (30)
Rnds 6–10 dc (5 rnds)
Rnd 11 (dc3, dc2tog) 6 times (24)
Rnd 12 dc
Rnd 13 (dc2, dc2tog) 6 times (18)
Rnd 14 (dc2tog) 9 times (9)

POD
Working in Green
Ch21 and work around the chain
Rnd 1 dc19, dc2 into next st along one side of chain, dc19, dc2 into next st along other side of chain (42)
Rnd 2 dc2 into next st, dc2, dc2 into next st, dc13, dc2 into next st, dc2, (dc2 into next st) twice, dc2, dc2 into next st, dc13, dc2 into next st, dc2, dc2 into next (50)
Rnd 3 (dc4, dc2 into next st) 10 times (60)
Rnd 4 (dc2 into next st, dc29) twice (62)
Rnds 5–10 dc (6 rnds)
Rnd 11 dc2tog, dc2, dc2tog, dc25, dc2tog, dc2, dc2tog, dc25 (58)

Rnd 12 (dc2tog) twice, dc25, (dc2tog) twice, dc25 (54)
Rnd 13 (dc2tog) twice, dc23, (dc2tog) twice, dc23 (50)
Rnd 14 dc

CALYX (make one)
Working in Green
Ch12 and sl st to join into a circle
Rnds 1–3 dc (3 rnds)
Rnd 4 (dc2tog) 3 times, dc6 (9)
Rnd 5 (dc1, dc2tog) 3 times (6)
Rnds 6–7 dc (2 rnds)
Rnd 8 (dc2tog, dc1) twice (4)

LEGS (make two)
Working in Green
Begin by dc6 into ring
Rnd 1 (dc2 into next st) 6 times (12)
Rnd 2 (dc1, dc2 into next st) 6 times (18)
Rnds 3–5 dc (3 rnds)
Rnd 6 (dc2tog) 6 times, dc6 (12)
Rnd 7 (dc2tog) 3 times, dc6 (9)
Rnds 8–15 dc (8 rnds)

Continues overleaf

MADE IN Lime and Green (overleaf in Chive)
YARN QUANTITIES 25g Pea, 25g Pod
TIME TO GROW Moderate
REQUIRES Just the basics!

SEWING UP

1. Stuff PEAS and gather final stitches to close.
2. Insert three PEAS into POD.
3. Sew CALYX into position at top of POD.
4. Stuff feet and sew top of LEGS flat perpendicular to foot, then sew into position on bottom of POD.
5. Embroider eyes onto PEAS with Black and Cream yarn, and add facial expressions as desired in Black yarn.

Cauliflower

The fluffiest of all cauliflowers, this slow-growing make has a texture all of its own. A character that's sure to enjoy a cuddle with anyone who's a fan of enjoying this vegetable with lashings of cheese sauce on Sundays.

BODY
The body is worked from the top down.
Working in Cream
Begin by dc6 into ring
Rnd 1 (dc2 into next st) 6 times (12 sts)
Rnd 2 (dc1, dc2 into next st) 6 times (18)
Rnd 3 (dc2, dc2 into next st) 6 times (24)
Rnd 4 (dc3, dc2 into next st) 6 times (30)
Rnd 5 (dc4, dc2 into next st) 6 times (36)
Rnd 6 (dc5, dc2 into next st) 6 times (42)
Rnd 7 (dc6, dc2 into next st) 6 times (48)
Rnd 8 (dc7, dc2 into next st) 6 times (54)
Rnd 9 dc
Rnd 10 (dc8, dc2 into next st) 6 times (60)
Rnd 11 dc
Rnd 12 (dc9, dc2 into next st) 6 times (66)
Rnd 13 dc
Rnd 14 (dc10, dc2 into next st) 6 times (72)
Rnd 15 dc
Rnd 16 (dc11, dc2 into next st) 6 times (78)
Rnds 17–34 dc (18 rnds)
Rnd 35 (dc11, dc2tog) 6 times (72)
Stuff and change to Green
Rnd 36 (dc2tog) 36 times (36)
Rnd 37 (dc4, dc2tog) 6 times (30)
Rnd 38 (dc3, dc2tog) 6 times (24)
Rnd 39 (dc2, dc2tog) 6 times (18)
Rnd 40 (dc1, dc2tog) 6 times (12)
Rnd 41 (dc2tog) 6 times (6)

Working in Cream
Cover top of BODY with ch5 CHAIN LOOPS
    (see page 107). Don't work loops on Green
    or last 6 rounds of Cream on underside
    of BODY.

LEAVES (make six)
Working in Green
Ch15, turn and work back down chain
    as follows:
Row 1 dc1, htr1, tr1, dtr2, ttr5, qtr4
Row 2 turn and dc14 back along stitches
    just worked
Continue on other side of chain
Row 3 dc1, htr1, tr1, dtr2, ttr5, qtr4
Row 4 turn and dc14 back along stitches
    just worked
Break yarn.

LEGS (make two)
Working in Green
Begin by dc6 into ring
Rnd 1 (dc2 into next st) 6 times (12)
Rnd 2 (dc1, dc2 into next st) 6 times (18)
Rnd 3 (dc2, dc2 into next st) 6 times (24)
Rnd 4 (dc3, dc2 into next st) 6 times (30)
Rnds 5–7 dc (3 rnds)
Rnd 8 (dc3, dc2tog) 3 times, dc15 (27)
Continues overleaf

MADE IN Cream and Green
YARN QUANTITIES 100g Body, 50g Foliage
TIME TO GROW Slow
REQUIRES htr, tr, dtr, ttr, qtr, colour change, chain loops

Rnd 9 (dc2, dc2tog) 3 times, dc15 (24)
Rnd 10 (dc2tog) 12 times (12)
Rnds 11–15 dc (5 rnds)

ARMS (make two)

Working in Green
Begin by dc6 into ring
Rnd 1 (dc2 into next st) 6 times (12)
Rnd 2 (dc1, dc2 into next st) 6 times (18)
Rnd 3 (dc2, dc2 into next st) 6 times (24)
Rnds 4–8 dc (5 rnds)
Rnd 9 dc6, (dc1, dc2tog) 6 times (18)
Rnd 10 dc6, (dc2tog) 6 times (12)
Rnds 11–22 dc (12 rnds)

SEWING UP

1. Gather final stitches of BODY to close.
2. Sew LEAVES into position on bottom of BODY by sewing six stitches along bottom of each LEAF into six stitches around colour change round.
3. Stuff feet and sew top of LEGS flat, then sew into position on bottom of BODY.
4. Stuff hands and sew tops of ARMS flat perpendicular to hand, then sew into position on sides of BODY at top of LEAVES.
5. Embroider eyes with Black and Cream yarn, and mouth with Black yarn.

CHAIN LOOPS

  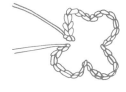

1   Insert the hook through the fabric at the desired position, yarn over and pull through the fabric.

2   Chain the number of stitches stated in the pattern.

3   Attach the chain to the fabric with a slip stitch approximately two stitches or two rounds away from the start of the chain. Repeat until the desired area is covered.

Courgette

Beginning as a gorgeous flower, the courgette is a fruit from the pumpkin family that grows on a plant with big green leaves and prickly stems. Make sure you've got plenty of space before planting a seed because it's one that will grow easily and abundantly and take over your whole patch.

BODY

The body is worked from the bottom up.
Working in Green
Begin by dc6 into ring
Rnd 1 (dc2 into next st) 6 times (12 sts)
Rnd 2 (dc1, dc2 into next st) 6 times (18)
Rnd 3 (dc2, dc2 into next st) 6 times (24)
Rnd 4 (dc3, dc2 into next st) 6 times (30)
Rnd 5 (dc4, dc2 into next st) 6 times (36)
Rnd 6 dc
Rnd 7 (dc5, dc2 into next st) 6 times (42)
Rnd 8 dc
Rnd 9 (dc6, dc2 into next st) 6 times (48)
Rnds 10–21 dc (12 rnds)
Rnd 22 (dc5, dc2tog) 3 times, dc27 (45)
Rnds 23–28 dc (6 rnds)
Rnd 29 (dc4, dc2tog) 3 times, (dc8, dc2 into next st) 3 times (45)
Rnds 30–32 dc (3 rnds)
Rnd 33 (dc3, dc2tog) 3 times, dc30 (42)
Rnds 34–45 dc (12 rnds)
Rnd 46 (dc2, dc2tog) 3 times, dc30 (39)
Rnds 47–49 dc (3 rnds)
Rnd 50 (dc2 into next st, dc5) 3 times, dc21 (42)
Rnds 51–53 dc (3 rnds)
Rnd 54 (dc5, dc2tog) 6 times (36)
Rnd 55 (dc4, dc2tog) 6 times (30)
Rnd 56 (dc3, dc2tog) 6 times (24)
Rnd 57 (dc2, dc2tog) 6 times (18)
Rnd 58 (dc2tog) 9 times (9)

STALK

Working in Green
Ch18 and sl st to join into a circle
Rnds 1–2 dc (2 rnds)
Rnd 3 tr
Rnds 4–5 (FPtr1, BPtr1) 9 times (2 rnds)

TOP

Working in Green
Begin by dc6 into ring
Rnd 1 (dc2 into next st) 6 times (12)
Rnd 2 (dc1, dc2 into next st) 6 times (18)

Join edge of TOP to starting chain of STALK with a round of dc from the top down.

LEGS (make two)

Working in Lime
Begin by dc6 into ring
Rnd 1 (dc2 into next st) 6 times (12)
Rnd 2 (dc1, dc2 into next st) 6 times (18)
Rnd 3 (dc2, dc2 into next st) 6 times (24)
Rnd 4 (dc3, dc2 into next st) 6 times (30)
Rnds 5–7 dc (3 rnds)
Continues overleaf

MADE IN Green and Lime
YARN QUANTITIES 50g Vegetable, 50g Limbs
TIME TO GROW Moderate
REQUIRES tr, front post/back post

Rnd 8 (dc3, dc2tog) 3 times, dc15 (27)
Rnd 9 (dc2, dc2tog) 3 times, dc15 (24)
Rnd 10 (dc2tog) 12 times (12)
Rnds 11–23 dc (13 rnds)

ARMS (make two)
Working in Lime
Begin by dc6 into ring
Rnd 1 (dc2 into next st) 6 times (12)
Rnd 2 (dc1, dc2 into next st) 6 times (18)
Rnd 3 (dc2, dc2 into next st) 6 times (24)
Rnds 4–8 dc (5 rnds)
Rnd 9 dc6, (dc1, dc2tog) 6 times (18)
Rnd 10 dc6, (dc2tog) 6 times (12)
Rnds 11–22 dc (12 rnds)

SEWING UP
1. Stuff BODY and gather final stitches to close.
2. Sew STALK into position on top of BODY by sewing around edge and then press to invert top of STALK.
3. Stuff feet and sew top of LEGS flat, then sew into position on bottom of body.
4. Stuff hands and sew tops of ARMS flat perpendicular to hand, then sew into position on sides of BODY.
5. Embroider eyes with Black and Cream yarn.

Chilli Pepper

There's a chilli pepper to suit everyone's taste, whether you like them bitter and green, sweet and yellow, or as flaming red as they come. A perfect plant for anyone without a garden, this will grow on a windowsill in full sun, and produce just as good a harvest of fiery fruits.

BODY

The body is worked from the top down.
Working in Ruby
Begin by dc6 into ring
Rnd 1 (dc2 into next st) 6 times (12 sts)
Rnd 2 (dc1, dc2 into next st) 6 times (18)
Rnd 3 (dc2, dc2 into next st) 6 times (24)
Rnd 4 (dc3, dc2 into next st) 6 times (30)
Rnd 5 (dc4, dc2 into next st) 6 times (36)
Rnd 6 dc
Rnd 7 (dc5, dc2 into next st) 6 times (42)
Rnds 8–23 dc (16 rnds)
Rnd 24 dc2tog, dc40 (41)
Rnd 25 dc
Rnd 26 dc2tog, dc39 (40)
Rnd 27 dc
Rnd 28 dc2tog, dc38 (39)
Rnd 29 dc
Rnd 30 dc2tog, dc37 (38)
Rnd 31 dc
Rnd 32 dc2tog, dc34, dc2tog (36)
Rnd 33 dc2tog, dc32, dc2tog (34)
Rnd 34 dc2tog, dc30, dc2tog (32)
Rnd 35 dc
Rnd 36 dc2tog, dc28, dc2tog (30)
Rnd 37 dc
Rnd 38 dc2tog, dc26, dc2tog (28)
Rnd 39 dc
Rnd 40 dc2tog, dc24, dc2tog (26)

Rnd 41 dc2tog, dc24 (25)
Rnd 42 dc2tog, dc23 (24)
Rnd 43 (dc2tog, dc6) 3 times (21)
Rnds 44–45 dc (2 rnds)
Rnd 46 dc10, (dc2tog) twice, dc7 (19)
Rnd 47 dc9, (dc2tog) twice, dc6 (17)
Rnd 48 dc
Rnd 49 dc9, dc2tog, dc6 (16)
Rnd 50 (dc2tog, dc2) 4 times (12)
Rnd 51 dc6, dc2tog, dc4 (11)
Rnd 52 dc6, dc2tog, dc3 (10)
Stuff and continue
Rnd 53 dc5, dc2tog, dc3 (9)
Rnd 54 (dc1, dc2tog) 3 times (6)
Rnd 55 (dc2tog, dc1) twice (4)

STALK

Working in Green
Begin by dc6 into ring
Rnd 1 (dc2 into next st) 6 times (12)
Rnd 2 htr
Rnd 3 (dc2, dc2tog) 3 times (9)
Rnds 4–5 dc (2 rnds)
Rnd 6 (dc1, dc2tog) 3 times (6)
Rnds 7–11 dc (5 rnds)
Rnd 12 (dc2 into next st) 3 times, dc1, dc2tog (8)
Rnd 13 dc4, (dc2tog) twice (6)
Continues overleaf

MADE IN Ruby and Green
YARN QUANTITIES 50g Body, 50g Foliage
TIME TO GROW Quick
REQUIRES htr

Rnds 14–17 dc (4 rnds)
Rnd 18 (dc2 into next st) 6 times (12)
Rnd 19 (dc1, dc2 into next st) 6 times (18)
Rnd 20 (dc2, dc2 into next st) 6 times (24)
Rnd 21 (dc3, htr2 into next st) 6 times (30)
Rnd 22 (dc4, htr1) 6 times

LEG (make one)
Working in Green
Begin by dc6 into ring
Rnd 1 (dc2 into next st) 6 times (12)
Rnd 2 (dc1, dc2 into next st) 6 times (18)
Rnd 3 (dc2, dc2 into next st) 6 times (24)
Rnd 4 (dc3, dc2 into next st) 6 times (30)
Rnds 5–7 dc (3 rnds)

Rnd 8 (dc3, dc2tog) 3 times, dc15 (27)
Rnd 9 (dc2, dc2tog) 3 times, dc15 (24)
Rnd 10 (dc2tog) 12 times (12)
Rnds 11–26 dc (16 rnds)

SEWING UP
1. Gather final stitches of BODY to close.
2. Stuff tip of STALK and sew to top of BODY by sewing around edge.
3. Stuff foot and sew top of LEG flat perpendicular to foot, then sew into position on side of BODY.
4. Embroider eyes with Black and Cream yarn, and mouth with Black yarn.

Corn on the Cob

Corn is a wild grass and this pattern is for an 'ear' of corn with each crocheted bobble representing a kernel. On average, a real ear of corn is made up of 800 kernels, so although this might feel like a slower make, at least you've only got 219 bobbles to make!

MLB
Make Large Bobble (through on fifth repeat)
(yarn over hook, insert hook into stitch, yarn over and bring through, yarn over and bring through first 2 loops) 4 times, yarn over hook, insert hook into stitch, yarn over and bring through, yarn over and bring through all loops on hook.

MSB
Make Small Bobble (through on fourth repeat)
(yarn over hook, insert hook into stitch, yarn over and bring through, yarn over and bring through first 2 loops) 3 times, yarn over hook, insert hook into stitch, yarn over and bring through, yarn over and bring through all loops on hook.

COB
Working in Lime
Begin by dc6 into ring
Rnd 1 (dc2 into next st) 6 times (12 sts)
Rnd 2 (dc1, dc2 into next st) 6 times (18)
Rnd 3 (dc2, dc2 into next st) 6 times (24)
Rnd 4 (dc3, dc2 into next st) 6 times (30)
Change to Yellow
Rnd 5 (dc4, dc2 into next st) 6 times (36)
Rnd 6 (dc5, dc2 into next st) 6 times (42)
Rnd 7 (MLB, dc2) 14 times
Rnd 8 dc

Rnd 9 (MLB, dc2) 14 times
Rnd 10 dc
Rnd 11 (dc1, MLB, dc1) 14 times
Rnd 12 dc
Rnd 13 (dc1, MLB, dc1) 14 times
Rnd 14 dc
Rnd 15 (dc2tog, MLB, dc2, MLB) 7 times (35)
Rnd 16 dc
Rnd 17 (dc1, MLB, dc2, MLB) 7 times
Rnd 18 dc
Rnd 19 (dc1, MLB, dc2, MLB) 7 times
Rnd 20 dc
Rnd 21 (dc1, MLB, dc2, MLB) 7 times
Rnd 22 dc
Rnd 23 (dc2, MLB, dc1, MLB) 7 times
Rnd 24 dc
Rnd 25 (dc2, MLB, dc1, MLB) 7 times
Rnd 26 dc
Rnd 27 (dc1, MLB, dc2, MLB) 7 times
Rnd 28 dc
Rnd 29 (dc1, MLB, dc2, MLB) 7 times
Rnd 30 dc
Rnd 31 (dc1, MLB, dc2tog, MLB) 7 times (28)
Rnd 32 dc
Rnd 33 (dc1, MSB) 14 times
Rnd 34 dc
Rnd 35 (dc2tog, MSB, dc1, MSB) 5 times, dc2tog, MSB (22)
Continues overleaf

MADE IN Yellow and Lime (overleaf in Primrose)
YARN QUANTITIES 50g Corn, 50g Husk
TIME TO GROW Slow
REQUIRES htr, tr, dtr, bobbles, colour change

Rnd 36 dc
Rnd 37 (dc2tog, MSB) 7 times, dc1 (15)
Rnd 38 dc
Rnd 39 (MSB, dc2tog) 5 times (10)
Rnd 40 dc

HUSK (make three)
Working in Lime
Ch31, turn and work back down chain as follows:
dc3, htr3, tr3, dtr21
Dc3 across post of dtr and work down other
    side of chain as follows:
ch3, dtr21, tr3, htr3, dc3
Continue working around edge as follows:
dc3, htr3, tr3, dtr21, dc9 back to other side
    (3 across post, 3 sts, 3 chains), ch3, dtr21, tr3,
    htr3, dc3
Break yarn.

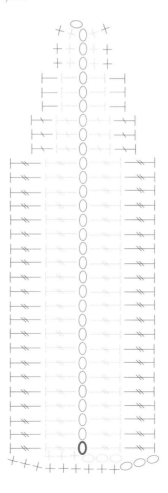

LEGS (make two)
Working in Lime
Begin by dc6 into ring
Rnd 1 (dc2 into next st) 6 times (12)
Rnd 2 (dc1, dc2 into next st) 6 times (18)
Rnd 3 (dc2, dc2 into next st) 6 times (24)
Rnd 4 (dc3, dc2 into next st) 6 times (30)
Rnds 5–7 dc (3 rnds)
Rnd 8 (dc3, dc2tog) 3 times, dc15 (27)
Rnd 9 (dc2, dc2tog) 3 times, dc15 (24)
Rnd 10 (dc2tog) 12 times (12)
Rnds 11–18 dc (8 rnds)

ARMS (make two)
Working in Lime
Begin by dc6 into ring
Rnd 1 (dc2 into next st) 6 times (12)
Rnd 2 (dc1, dc2 into next st) 6 times (18)
Rnd 3 (dc2, dc2 into next st) 6 times (24)
Rnds 4–8 dc (5 rnds)
Rnd 9 dc6, (dc1, dc2tog) 6 times (18)
Rnd 10 dc6, (dc2tog) 6 times (12)
Rnds 11–22 dc (12 rnds)

SEWING UP
1. Stuff COB and gather final stitches to close.
2. Sew three HUSK pieces onto colour change
   line on bottom of BODY.
3. Secure HUSK as desired by sewing into
   place up length of COB.
4. Stuff feet and sew top of LEGS flat, then sew
   into position towards front of bottom circle.
5. Stuff hands and sew top of ARMS flat, then
   sew into position on COB on top of HUSK.
6. Embroider eyes with Black and Cream yarn.

Cherry Tomato

This easy to grow, prolific plant provides the perfect post-chore or mid-game garden snack for the whole family. Hook these crocheted versions up on the vine to make them line dance, creating hours of entertainment, or make them individually as the perfect mascot for any gardener.

BODY (make up to three)

Working in Ruby
Begin by dc6 into ring
Rnd 1 (dc2 into next st) 6 times (12 sts)
Rnd 2 (dc1, dc2 into next st) 6 times (18)
Rnd 3 (dc2, dc2 into next st) 6 times (24)
Rnd 4 (dc3, dc2 into next st) 6 times (30)
Rnd 5 (dc4, dc2 into next st) 6 times (36)
Rnd 6 dc
Rnd 7 (dc5, dc2 into next st) 6 times (42)
Rnds 8–9 dc (2 rnds)
Rnd 10 (dc6, dc2 into next st) 6 times (48)
Rnd 11–15 dc (5 rnds)
Rnd 16 (dc2tog, dc6) 6 times (42)
Rnd 17 dc
Rnd 18 (dc2tog, dc5) 6 times (36)
Rnd 19 dc
Rnd 20 (dc2tog, dc4) 6 times (30)
Rnd 21 (dc2tog, dc3) 6 times (24)
Rnd 22 (dc2tog, dc2) 6 times (18)
Rnd 23 (dc2tog) 9 times (9)
Stuff and continue
Rnd 24 (dc2tog, dc1) 3 times (6)
Rnd 25 dc

SEPAL (make one per tomato)

Working in Green
Begin by dc10 into ring

*Ch6, turn and work back down chain as follows:
sl st2, dc2, htr1, sl st2 along rnd
Repeat from * 4 more times
Break yarn.

LEGS (make two per tomato)

Working in Green
Begin by dc6 into ring
Rnd 1 (dc2 into next st) 6 times (12)
Continues overleaf

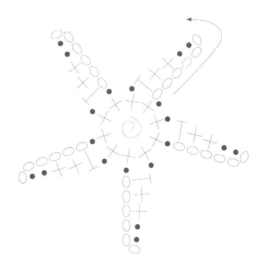

MADE IN Ruby and Green
YARN QUANTITIES 50g Fruit, 50g Foliage (makes up to three tomatoes and vine)
TIME TO GROW Quick
REQUIRES htr

Rnd 2 (dc1, dc2 into next st) 6 times (18)
Rnds 3–5 dc (3 rnds)
Rnd 6 (dc2tog) 6 times, dc6 (12)
Rnd 7 (dc2tog) 3 times, dc6 (9)
Rnds 8–15 dc (8 rnds)

VINE (make one)
Working in Green
Begin by dc6 into ring
Rnds 1–50 dc (50 rnds)
Break yarn.

SEWING UP
1. Gather final stitches of BODY to close. Sew directly through central ring, pull tight and fasten off at bottom to invert top.

2. Sew in ends on SEPAL and then sew into position into indent where last piece finished. Tack point of each leaf down.
3. Stuff feet and sew tops of LEGS flat, then sew into position at bottom of BODY.
4. Embroider eyes on each with Black and Cream yarn, and mouth with Black yarn.

OPTIONAL
Attach each tomato to alternate sides of VINE as follows:
sl st into top of SEPAL, ch10 and sl st into VINE
Row 1 work a row of dc10 back along chain, sl st into SEPAL
Row 2 turn and dc10, sl st into VINE
Break yarn.

Bell Pepper

Sweetening as they ripen, these peppers look best made and displayed in a trio of shades from bitter green through to ruby red. In addition to these commonly seen colours, the Bell Pepper can also be grown in purple, white and brown.

BODY
The body is worked from the bottom up.
Working in Yellow
Begin by dc6 into ring
Rnd 1 (dc2 into next st) 6 times (12 sts)
Rnd 2 (dc1, (dc2 into next st) twice, dc1) 3 times (18)
Rnd 3 (dc1, (dc2 into next st) 4 times, dc1) 3 times (30)
Rnd 4 (dc2tog, dc8) 3 times (27)
Rnd 5 (dc4, dc2 into next st, dc4) 3 times (30)
Rnd 6 (dc4, dc2 into next st) 6 times (36)
Rnds 7–8 dc (2 rnds)
Rnd 9 (dc5, dc2 into next st) 6 times (42)
Rnd 10 dc
Rnd 11 (dc6, dc2 into next st) 6 times (48)
Rnds 12–14 dc (3 rnds)
Rnd 15 (dc7, dc2 into next st) 6 times (54)
Rnds 16–18 dc (3 rnds)
Rnd 19 (dc8, dc2 into next st) 6 times (60)
Rnds 20–27 dc (8 rnds)
Rnd 28 (dc4, dc2 into next st) 6 times, dc30 (66)
Rnd 29 dc
Rnd 30 (dc2 into next st, dc10) 6 times (72)
Rnds 31–33 dc (3 times)
Rnd 34 (dc2tog, dc2tog, dc8) 6 times (60)
Rnd 35 (dc2tog, dc8) 6 times (54)
Rnd 36 (dc2tog, dc7) 6 times (48)
Rnd 37 (dc2tog, dc6) 6 times (42)
Rnd 38 (dc2tog, dc5) 6 times (36)
Rnd 39 (dc2tog, dc4) 6 times (30)
Rnd 40 (dc2tog, dc3) 6 times (24)
Rnd 41 (dc2tog) 12 times (12)
Stuff and continue
Rnd 42 (dc2, dc2tog) 3 times (9)
Rnd 43 dc
Rnd 44 (dc1, dc2tog) 3 times (6)
Break yarn, leaving long end for sewing up.

STALK
Working in Green
Begin by dc6 into ring
Rnd 1 (dc2 into next st) 6 times (12)
Rnd 2 htr
Rnds 3–11 dc (9 rnds)
Rnd 12 (dc2 into next st) 3 times, dc1, (dc2tog) 4 times (11)
Rnds 13–15 dc (3 rnds)
Rnd 16 dc10, dc2 into next st (12)
Rnd 17 (dc1, dc2 into next st) 6 times (18)
Rnd 18 (dc2, htr2 into next st) 6 times (24)

LEGS (make two)
Working in Green
Begin by dc6 into ring
Rnd 1 (dc2 into next st) 6 times (12)
Rnd 2 (dc1, dc2 into next st) 6 times (18)
Rnd 3 (dc2, dc2 into next st) 6 times (24)
Rnd 4 (dc3, dc2 into next st) 6 times (30)
Continues overleaf

MADE IN Yellow and Green
YARN QUANTITIES 50g Fruit, 50g Foliage
TIME TO GROW Moderate
REQUIRES htr

124

Rnds 5–7 dc (3 rnds)
Rnd 8 (dc3, dc2tog) 3 times, dc15 (27)
Rnd 9 (dc2, dc2tog) 3 times, dc15 (24)
Rnd 10 (dc2tog) 12 times (12)
Rnds 11–23 dc (13 rnds)

ARMS (make two)
Working in Green
Begin by dc6 into ring
Rnd 1 (dc2 into next st) 6 times (12)
Rnd 2 (dc1, dc2 into next st) 6 times (18)
Rnd 3 (dc2, dc2 into next st) 6 times (24)
Rnds 4–8 dc (5 rnds)
Rnd 9 dc6, (dc1, dc2tog) 6 times (18)
Rnd 10 dc6, (dc2tog) 6 times (12)
Rnds 11–22 dc (12 rnds)

SEWING UP
1. Gather final stitches of BODY to close and invert both top and bottom by sewing through both ends and pulling tight.
2. Stuff STEM and sew into position on top of BODY by sewing two rounds in from edge of STEM (this leaves the edge sitting slightly off the fabric).
3. Stuff feet and sew tops of LEGS flat perpendicular to foot, then sew into position on bottom of BODY.
4. Stuff hands and sew tops of ARMS flat perpendicular to hand, then sew into position on sides of BODY.
5. Embroider eyes with Black and Cream yarn.

Butternut Squash

Another fruit masquerading as a vegetable, the Butternut Squash can be roasted, mashed, steamed, grilled or fried. This pattern is as easy to make as a squash is to grow in your garden, and it makes a great addition to any autumnal decorations in your home.

BODY

The body is worked from the bottom up.
Working in Oatmeal
Begin by dc6 into ring
Rnd 1 (dc2 into next st) 6 times (12 sts)
Rnd 2 (dc1, dc2 into next st) 6 times (18)
Rnd 3 (dc2, dc2 into next st) 6 times (24)
Rnd 4 (dc3, dc2 into next st) 6 times (30)
Rnd 5 (dc4, dc2 into next st) 6 times (36)
Rnd 6 (dc5, dc2 into next st) 6 times (42)
Rnd 7 (dc6, dc2 into next st) 6 times (48)
Rnd 8 (dc7, dc2 into next st) 6 times (54)
Rnd 9 (dc8, dc2 into next st) 6 times (60)
Rnd 10 dc
Rnd 11 (dc9, dc2 into next st) 6 times (66)
Rnd 12 dc
Rnd 13 (dc10, dc2 into next st) 6 times (72)
Rnds 14–19 dc (6 rnds)
Rnd 20 (dc10, dc2tog) 6 times (66)
Rnd 21 dc
Rnd 22 (dc9, dc2tog) 6 times (60)
Rnd 23 (dc8, dc2tog) 6 times (54)
Rnd 24 (dc7, dc2tog) 6 times (48)
Rnds 25–26 dc (2 rnds)
Rnd 27 (dc6, dc2tog) 6 times (42)
Rnds 28–47 dc (20 rnds)
Rnd 48 (dc5, dc2tog) 6 times (36)
Rnd 49 dc
Rnd 50 (dc4, dc2tog) 6 times (30)

Rnd 51 (dc3, dc2tog) 6 times (24)
Rnd 52 (dc2, dc2tog) 6 times (18)
Rnd 53 (dc1, dc2tog) 6 times (12)
Rnd 54 (dc2, dc2tog) 3 times (9)

STALK

Working in Fudge
Ch18 and sl st to join into a circle
Rnd 1 dc
Rnd 2 tr
Rnd 3 (FPtr1, BPtr1) 9 times
Rnd 4 (dc3tog) 6 times (6)
Rnds 5–8 dc (4 rnds)

LEGS (MAKE TWO)

Working in Fudge
Begin by dc6 into ring
Rnd 1 (dc2 into next st) 6 times (12)
Rnd 2 (dc1, dc2 into next st) 6 times (18)
Rnd 3 (dc2, dc2 into next st) 6 times (24)
Rnd 4 (dc3, dc2 into next st) 6 times (30)
Rnds 5–7 dc (3 rnds)
Rnd 8 (dc3, dc2tog) 3 times, dc15 (27)
Rnd 9 (dc2, dc2tog) 3 times, dc15 (24)
Rnd 10 (dc2tog) 12 times (12)
Rnds 11–23 dc (13 rnds)

Continues overleaf

MADE IN Oatmeal and Fudge
YARN QUANTITIES 50g Vegetable, 25g Foliage
TIME TO GROW Moderate
REQUIRES tr, front post/back post

SEWING UP

1. Stuff BODY and gather final stitches to close.
2. Gather final stitches to close STALK and sew into position on top of BODY.
3. Stuff feet and sew the top of LEGS flat, then sew into position on bottom of BODY.
4. Embroider eyes with Black and Cream yarn.

Okra

An edible seed pod, okra develops from a beautiful flowering plant, but it would need a long, hot summer to bear fruit here in the UK. This pattern is one of the most unusual in the book, but as a result it's a very satisfying make.

Note: The front post htr in this pattern are not counted as a stitch in the stitch counts.

BODY

The body is worked from the top down.
Working in Green
Begin by dc5 into ring
Rnd 1 (dc2 into next st) 5 times (10 sts)
Rnd 2 (ch3 and sl st 1, dc1 back down chain, dc2 along rnd) 5 times (5 spikes)
Rnd 3 (dc2 along chain, dc2 into next st, dc3) 5 times (35)
Rnd 4 (dc2, (dc2 into next st) twice, dc3) 5 times (45)
Rnd 5 (dc4, htr2 into next st, dc4) 5 times (50)
Rnd 6 (dc5, htr1 around post of same htr below, dc5) 5 times (50)
Rnds 7–16 (dc5, htr1 around post of htr below, dc5) 5 times (10 rnds)
Rnd 17 dc5, (htr1 around post of htr below, dc3, dc3tog, dc4) 4 times, htr1 around post of htr below, dc3, dc3tog across rnd and move marker to this point (40)
Rnds 18–27 (dc4, htr1 around post of htr below, dc4) 5 times (10 rnds)
Rnd 28 dc4, (htr1 around post of htr below, dc2, dc3tog, dc3) 4 times, htr1 around post of htr below, dc2, dc3tog across rnd and move marker to this point (30)
Rnds 29–33 (dc3, htr1 around post of htr below, dc3) 5 times (5 rnds)
Rnd 34 dc3, (htr1 around post of htr below, dc1, dc3tog, dc2) 4 times, htr1 around post of htr below, dc1, dc3tog across rnd and move marker to this point (20)
Rnds 35–39 (dc2, htr1 around post of htr below, dc2) 5 times (5 rnds)
Rnd 40 dc2, (htr1 around post of htr below, dc3tog, dc1) 4 times, htr1 around post of htr below, dc3tog across rnd and move marker to this point (10)
Rnds 41–43 (dc1, htr1 around post of htr below, dc1) 5 times (3 rnds)
Stuff and continue
Rnd 44 dc1, (htr1 around post of htr below, dc2tog) 4 times, htr1 around post of htr below, dc2tog across rnd and move marker to this point (5)
Rnd 45 htr1 around htr posts (5 times)

STALK

Working in Green
Begin by dc6 into ring
Rnd 1 (dc1, dc2 into next st) 3 times (9)
Rnd 2 htr
Rnds 3–5 dc (3 rnds)
Rnd 6 (dc2, dc2 into next st) 3 times (12)
Rnds 7–9 dc (3 rnds)
Rnd 10 (dc3, dc2 into next st) 3 times (15)
Rnd 11 (dc4, dc2 into next st) 3 times (18)
Continues overleaf

MADE IN Green and Lime
YARN QUANTITIES 50g Vegetable, 25g Limbs
TIME TO GROW Moderate
REQUIRES htr, front post

Rnd 12 (dc2, dc2 into next st) 6 times (24)
Rnd 13 dc
Rnd 14 (dc3, dc2 into next st) 6 times (30)
Rnd 15 dc

LEGS (make two)
Working in Lime
Begin by dc6 into ring
Rnd 1 (dc2 into next st) 6 times (12)
Rnd 2 (dc1, dc2 into next st) 6 times (18)
Rnd 3 (dc2, dc2 into next st) 6 times (24)
Rnd 4 (dc3, dc2 into next st) 6 times (30)
Rnds 5–7 dc (3 rnds)
Rnd 8 (dc3, dc2tog) 3 times, dc15 (27)
Rnd 9 (dc2, dc2tog) 3 times, dc15 (24)
Rnd 10 (dc2tog) 12 times (12)
Rnds 11–28 dc (18 rnds)

ARMS (make two)
Working in Lime
Begin by dc6 into ring

Rnd 1 (dc2 into next st) 6 times (12)
Rnd 2 (dc1, dc2 into next st) 6 times (18)
Rnd 3 (dc2, dc2 into next st) 6 times (24)
Rnds 4–8 dc (5 rnds)
Rnd 9 dc6, (dc1, dc2tog) 6 times (18)
Rnd 10 dc6, (dc2tog) 6 times (12)
Rnds 11–22 dc (12 rnds)

SEWING UP
1. Gather final stitches of BODY to close.
2. Stuff STALK and sew into position on top of BODY.
3. Stuff feet and sew tops of LEGS flat perpendicular to foot, then sew into position on sides of body.
4. Stuff hands and sew tops of ARMS flat perpendicular to hand, then sew into position on sides of BODY.
5. Embroider eyes with Black and Cream yarn.

Pumpkin

There are hundreds of varieties of edible pumpkin, from the classic orange to white and blue. The season most associated with these large fruits is Halloween, and this pattern can be easily adapted into a jack-o-lantern with additional black embroidery in place of the eyes.

BODY

The body is worked from the bottom up.
Working in Orange
Begin by dc6 into ring
Rnd 1 (dc2 into next st) 6 times (12 sts)
Rnd 2 (dc1, dc2 into next st) 6 times (18)
Rnd 3 (dc2, dc2 into next st) 6 times (24)
Rnd 4 (dc3, dc2 into next st) 6 times (30)
Rnd 5 (dc4, dc2 into next st) 6 times (36)
Rnd 6 (dc5, dc2 into next st) 6 times (42)
Rnd 7 (dc6, dc2 into next st) 6 times (48)
Rnd 8 (dc7, dc2 into next st) 6 times (54)
Rnd 9 (dc8, dc2 into next st) 6 times (60)
Rnd 10 (dc9, dc2 into next st) 6 times (66)
Rnd 11 (dc10, dc2 into next st) 6 times (72)
Rnd 12 (dc11, dc2 into next st) 6 times (78)
Rnd 13 dc
Rnd 14 (dc12, dc2 into next st) 6 times (84)
Rnd 15 dc
Rnd 16 (dc13, dc2 into next st) 6 times (90)
Rnds 17–36 dc (20 rnds)
Rnd 37 (dc13, dc2tog) 6 times (84)
Rnd 38 dc
Rnd 39 (dc12, dc2tog) 6 times (78)
Rnd 40 dc
Rnd 41 (dc11, dc2tog) 6 times (72)
Rnd 42 (dc10, dc2tog) 6 times (66)
Rnd 43 (dc9, dc2tog) 6 times (60)
Rnd 44 (dc8, dc2tog) 6 times (54)

Rnd 45 (dc7, dc2tog) 6 times (48)
Rnd 46 (dc6, dc2tog) 6 times (42)
Rnd 47 (dc5, dc2tog) 6 times (36)
Rnd 48 (dc4, dc2tog) 6 times (30)
Rnd 49 dc
Rnd 50 (dc3, dc2tog) 6 times (24)
Rnd 51 dc
Rnd 52 (dc2, dc2tog) 6 times (18)
Rnds 53–54 dc (2 rnds)
Stuff and continue
Rnd 55 (dc2tog) 9 times (9)
Rnd 56 dc
Rnd 57 (dc1, dc2tog) 3 times (6)

STALK

Working in Green
Begin by dc6 into ring
Rnd 1 (dc2 into next st) 6 times (12)
Rnd 2 (dc2, dc2 into next st) 4 times (16)
Rnd 3 tr
Rnds 4–5 (FPtr1, BPtr1) 8 times (2 rnds)
Rnd 6 (FPtr1, miss back post) 8 times (8)
Rnds 7–11 (FPtr1) 8 times (5 rnds)
Rnd 12 (dc3, dc2 into next st) twice (10)
Rnd 13 (ch5, turn and dc2, htr2 back down chain, dc2 along rnd) 5 times

Continues overleaf

MADE IN Orange and Green
YARN QUANTITIES 75g Fruit, 25g Foliage
TIME TO GROW Slow
REQUIRES htr, tr, front post/back post, slip stitch traverse

LEGS (make two)

Working in Green

Begin by dc6 into ring

Rnd 1 (dc2 into next st) 6 times (12)
Rnd 2 (dc1, dc2 into next st) 6 times (18)
Rnd 3 (dc2, dc2 into next st) 6 times (24)
Rnd 4 (dc3, dc2 into next st) 6 times (30)
Rnds 5–7 dc (3 rnds)
Rnd 8 (dc3, dc2tog) 3 times, dc15 (27)
Rnd 9 (dc2, dc2tog) 3 times, dc15 (24)
Rnd 10 (dc2tog) 12 times (12)
Rnds 11–23 dc (13 rnds)

SEWING UP

1. Gather final stitches of BODY to close. Sew directly through central ring, pull tight and fasten off at bottom to invert top.
2. Working in Orange, work SLIP STITCH TRAVERSE (see page 28) in lines from bottom to top to create six segments.
3. Sew STALK into position on top of BODY by sewing around the dc round at bottom (this leaves the points sitting off the fabric).
4. Work three TENDRILS onto bottom edge of stalk as below.
5. Stuff feet and sew top of LEGS flat, then sew into position on bottom of body.
6. Embroider eyes with Black and Cream yarn.

TENDRILS

Working in Green

SHORT (make two)

Sl st into position at bottom of stalk, ch41, turn and work back down chain as follows:
(sl st2, sl st2tog) 10 times (30)

LONG (make one)

Sl st into position at bottom of stalk, ch81, turn and work back down chain as follows:
(sl st2, sl st2tog) 20 times (60)

Broccoli

This crochet pattern is for a single floret of broccoli, topped off with a texture that captures the appearance of its unopened flower buds. Broccoli resembles little trees and it's a popular first food eaten by weaning babies, due to its fun shape and its distinctive taste.

STALK

The stalk is worked from the bottom up.
Working in Lime
Ch42 and sl st to join into a circle
Rnds 1–5 dc (5 rnds)
Rnd 6 (dc5, dc2tog) 6 times (36)
Rnds 7–16 dc (10 rnds)
Rnd 17 (dc4, dc2tog) 6 times (30)
Rnds 18–22 dc (5 rnds)
Rnd 23 (dc4, dc2 into next st) 6 times (36)
Continue as follows to create three 24-st rounds for the stems:
Ch12, miss 12 sts and sl st into next st
Dc11, ch6 and sl st to centre of other chain
Dc6 back down first chain towards stitch marker
Dc12 from main round, dc6 from chain

Continue in Lime and work each 24-st rnd as follows:
Rnds 1–2 dc (2 rnds)
Rnd 3 (dc6, dc2tog) 3 times (21)
Rnds 4–6 dc (3 rnds)
Rnd 7 (dc5, dc2tog) 3 times (18)
Rnds 8–12 dc (5 rnds)
Change to Green
Rnd 13 (dc2, dc2 into next st) 6 times (24)
Break yarn. Rejoin in centre and repeat for second and third stems.

BASE

Working in Lime
Begin by dc6 into ring
Rnd 1 (dc2 into next st) 6 times (12)
Rnd 2 (dc1, dc2 into next st) 6 times (18)
Rnd 3 (dc2, dc2 into next st) 6 times (24)
Rnd 4 (dc3, dc2 into next st) 6 times (30)
Rnd 5 (dc4, dc2 into next st) 6 times (36)
Rnd 6 (dc5, dc2 into next st) 6 times (42)

LARGE TOP

Working in Green
Begin by dc6 into ring
Rnd 1 (dc2 into next st) 6 times (12)
Rnd 2 (dc1, dc2 into next st) 6 times (18)
Rnd 3 (dc2, dc2 into next st) 6 times (24)
Rnd 4 (dc3, dc2 into next st) 6 times (30)
Rnd 5 (dc4, dc2 into next st) 6 times (36)
Rnd 6 (dc5, dc2 into next st) 6 times (42)
Rnd 7 (dc6, dc2 into next st) 6 times (48)
Rnd 8 (dc7, dc2 into next st) 6 times (54)
Rnd 9 (dc8, dc2 into next st) 6 times (60)
Rnd 10 (dc9, dc2 into next st) 6 times (66)
Rnd 11 dc
Rnd 12 (dc10, dc2 into next st) 6 times (72)
Rnd 13 dc
Rnd 14 (dc11, dc2 into next st) 6 times (78)
Rnds 15–16 dc (2 rnds)
Continues overleaf

MADE IN Green and Lime
YARN QUANTITIES 75g Top, 50g Stalk
TIME TO GROW Slow
REQUIRES Chain loops, chain split, colour change

Rnd 17 (dc11, dc2tog) 6 times (72)
Rnd 18 (dc10, dc2tog) 6 times (66)
Rnd 19 (dc9, dc2tog) 6 times (60)
Rnd 20 (dc8, dc2tog) 6 times (54)
Rnd 21 (dc7, dc2tog) 6 times (48)
Rnd 22 (dc6, dc2tog) 6 times (42)
Rnd 23 (dc5, dc2tog) 6 times (36)
Rnd 24 (dc4, dc2tog) 6 times (30)
Rnd 25 (dc3, dc2tog) 6 times (24)
Rnd 26 (dc2, dc2tog) 6 times (18)
Rnd 27 (dc1, dc2tog) 6 times (12)
Rnd 28 (dc2, dc2tog) 3 times (9)
Stuff and gather sts to close. Sew in end.

SMALL TOP

Working in Green
Begin by dc6 into ring
Rnd 1 (dc2 into next st) 6 times (12)
Rnd 2 (dc1, dc2 into next st) 6 times (18)
Rnd 3 (dc2, dc2 into next st) 6 times (24)
Rnd 4 dc
Rnd 5 (dc3, dc2 into next st) 6 times (30)
Rnd 6 dc
Rnd 7 (dc4, dc2 into next st) 6 times (36)
Rnds 8–9 dc (2 rnds)
Rnd 10 (dc4, dc2tog) 6 times (30)
Rnd 11 (dc3, dc2tog) 6 times (24)
Rnd 12 (dc2, dc2tog) 6 times (18)
Rnd 13 (dc1, dc2tog) 6 times (12)
Rnd 14 (dc2tog) 6 times (6)
Stuff and gather sts to close. Sew in end.

Working in Green
Cover top half of both LARGE TOP and
   SMALL TOP with ch8 CHAIN LOOPS
   (see page 107), leaving undersides blank.

LEGS (make two)

Working in Lime
Begin by dc6 into ring
Rnd 1 (dc2 into next st) 6 times (12)
Rnd 2 (dc1, dc2 into next st) 6 times (18)
Rnd 3 (dc2, dc2 into next st) 6 times (24)
Rnd 4 (dc3, dc2 into next st) 6 times (30)
Rnds 5–7 dc (3 rnds)
Rnd 8 (dc3, dc2tog) 3 times, dc15 (27)
Rnd 9 (dc2, dc2tog) 3 times, dc15 (24)
Rnd 10 (dc2tog) 12 times (12)
Rnds 11–18 dc (8 rnds)

SEWING UP

1. Stuff STALK and join BASE to STALK with a
   round of dc from the bottom up in Lime.
2. Sew top of each stem closed.
3. Sew LARGE TOP into position on two stems.
4. Sew SMALL TOP into position on third stem.
5. Stuff foot and sew the top of LEGS flat, then
   sew into position onto joining edge of base.
6. Embroider eyes with Black and Cream yarn.

Garlic

A heavyweight for flavour, garlic can be easily grown by planting a single clove quite deep into the soil, with the flat end downwards. Crochet a whole bulb with three sprouting shoots as the perfect gift for any foodie.

BULB

The body is worked from the bottom up.
Working in Cream
Begin by dc6 into ring
Rnd 1 (dc2 into next st) 6 times (12 sts)
Rnd 2 (dc1, dc2 into next st) 6 times (18)
Rnd 3 (dc2, dc2 into next st) 6 times (24)
Rnd 4 (dc3, dc2 into next st) 6 times (30)
Working into back loop only
Rnd 5 (dc4, dc2 into next st) 6 times (36)
Continue working through whole stitch
Rnd 6 (dc2 into next st) 36 times (72)
Rnds 7–12 dc (6 rnds)
Rnd 13 (dc2tog, dc10) 6 times (66)
Rnd 14 dc
Rnd 15 (dc2tog, dc9) 6 times (60)
Rnds 16–18 dc (3 rnds)
Rnd 19 (dc2tog, dc8) 6 times (54)
Rnds 20–24 dc (5 rnds)
Rnd 25 (dc2tog, dc7) 6 times (48)
Rnd 26 (dc2tog, dc6) 6 times (42)
Rnd 27 (dc2tog, dc5) 6 times (36)
Rnd 28 (dc2tog, dc4) 6 times (30)
Rnds 29–30 dc (2 rnds)
Rnd 31 (dc3, dc2tog) 6 times (24)
Rnd 32 (dc2, dc2tog) 6 times (18)
Rnds 33–35 dc (3 rnds)
Rnd 36 (dc2tog, dc4) 3 times (15)
Rnd 37 (dc1, dc2 into next st) 3 times,
   (dc1, dc2tog) 3 times (15)

Rnd 38 dc
Break yarn and leave long end for sewing up.

SHORT SHOOT (make one)

Working in Lime
Begin by dc6 into ring
Rnd 1 (dc2 into next st) 6 times (12)
Rnd 2 dc
Rnd 3 (dc3, dc2 into next st) 3 times (15)
Rnds 4–13 dc (10 rnds)
Rnd 14 (dc3, dc2tog) 3 times (12)
Rnd 15 (dc2, dc2tog) 3 times (9)
Rnd 16 (dc1, dc2tog) 3 times (6)

LONG SHOOT (make one)

Working in Lime
Begin by dc6 into ring
Rnd 1 (dc2 into next st) 6 times (12)
Rnd 2 dc
Rnd 3 (dc3, dc2 into next st) 3 times (15)
Rnds 4–15 dc (12 rnds)
Rnd 16 (dc3, dc2tog) 3 times (12)
Rnd 17 (dc2, dc2tog) 3 times (9)
Rnd 18 (dc1, dc2tog) 3 times (6)

LEGS (make two)

Working in Lime
Begin by dc6 into ring
Rnd 1 (dc2 into next st) 6 times (12)
Continues overleaf

MADE IN Cream and Lime
YARN QUANTITIES 50g Bulb, 25g Foliage
TIME TO GROW Moderate
REQUIRES Back loop, slip stitch traverse

Rnd 2 (dc1, dc2 into next st) 6 times (18)
Rnd 3 (dc2, dc2 into next st) 6 times (24)
Rnd 4 (dc3, dc2 into next st) 6 times (30)
Rnds 5–7 dc (3 rnds)
Rnd 8 (dc3, dc2tog) 3 times, dc15 (27)
Rnd 9 (dc2, dc2tog) 3 times, dc15 (24)
Rnd 10 (dc2tog) 12 times (12)
Rnds 11–23 dc (13 rnds)

SEWING UP

1. Stuff BULB and leave top of BULB open.
   Do not sew in end yet.

2. Sew two SHOOTS together at bottom.
3. Insert SHOOTS into open top of BULB and
   sew into place using the Cream yarn end.
4. Stuff feet and sew top of LEGS flat, then sew
   into position on bottom of BULB.
5. Finish by working SLIP STITCH TRAVERSE
   (see page 28) in lines from bottom to top to
   create six segments.
6. Embroider eyes with Black and Cream yarn.

Rainbow Chard

A perfect beginner project, with just as much character as the most advanced one, this colourful make will brighten up any kitchen shelf. Crunchier than spinach, but more tender than kale, this stunning leafy vegetable comes in a surprising array of shades.

BODY

The body is worked from the top down.
Working in Magenta
Begin by dc6 into ring
Rnds 1–3 dc (3 rnds)
Rnd 4 dc2 into next st, dc5 (7)
Rnds 5–6 dc (2 rnds)
Rnd 7 dc2 into next st, dc6 (8)
Rnds 8–9 dc (2 rnds)
Rnd 10 dc2 into next st, dc7 (9)
Rnds 11–13 dc (3 rnds)
Rnd 14 dc2 into next st, dc8 (10)
Rnds 15–17 dc (3 rnds)
Rnd 18 dc2 into next st, dc9 (11)
Rnds 19–21 dc (3 rnds)
Rnd 22 dc2 into next st, dc10 (12)
Rnd 23 dc
Rnd 24 (dc3, dc2 into next st) 3 times (15)
Rnds 25–27 dc (3 rnds)
Rnd 28 (dc4, dc2 into next st) 3 times (18)
Rnds 29–31 dc (3 rnds)
Rnd 32 (dc5, dc2 into next st) 3 times (21)
Rnds 33–35 dc (3 rnds)
Rnd 36 (dc6, dc2 into next st) 3 times (24)
Rnd 37 dc
Rnd 38 (dc7, dc2 into next st) 3 times (27)
Rnd 39 dc
Rnd 40 (dc8, dc2 into next st) 3 times (30)
Rnds 41–43 dc (3 rnds)

Rnd 44 (dc4, dc2 into next st) 6 times (36)
Rnds 45–47 dc (3 rnds)

BASE (see diagram overleaf)

Working in Magenta
Ch11 and work around the chain
Rnd 1 dc9, dc2 into next st along one side of chain, dc9, dc2 into next st along other side of chain (22)
Rnd 2 dc2 into next st, dc8, dc2 into next st, dc1, dc2 into next st, dc8, dc2 into next st, dc1 (26)
Rnd 3 dc1, dc2 into next st, dc8, dc2 into next st, dc3, dc2 into next st, dc8, dc2 into next st, dc2 (30)
Rnd 4 (dc4, dc2 into next st) 6 times (36)

LEAF

Working in Green
Begin by dc6 into ring
Rnd 1 (dc2 into next st) 6 times (12)
Rnd 2 (dc1, dc2 into next st) 6 times (18)
Rnds 3–5 dc (3 rnds)
Rnd 6 dc2 into next st, dc7, (dc2 into next st) twice, dc7, dc2 into next st (22)
Rnd 7 dc2 into next st, dc9, (dc2 into next st) twice, dc9, dc2 into next st (26)

Continues overleaf

MADE IN Magenta and Green (overleaf in Yellow and Kale)
YARN QUANTITIES 50g Body, 50g Leaf
TIME TO GROW Moderate
REQUIRES Just the basics!

Rnd 8 dc2 into next st, dc11, (dc2 into next st) twice, dc11, dc2 into next st (30)

Rnd 9 dc2 into next st, dc13, (dc2 into next st) twice, dc13, dc2 into next st (34)

Rnd 10 dc2 into next st, dc15, (dc2 into next st) twice, dc15, dc2 into next st (38)

Rnds 11–15 dc (5 rnds)

Rnd 16 dc2tog, dc15, (dc2tog) twice, dc15, dc2tog (34)

Rnds 17–18 dc (2 rnds)

Rnd 19 dc2 into next st, dc15, (dc2 into next st) twice, dc15, dc2 into next st (38)

Rnd 20 dc2 into next st, dc17, (dc2 into next st) twice, dc17, dc2 into next st (42)

Rnd 21 (dc2 into next st) twice, dc19, (dc2 into next st) twice, dc19 (46)

Rnds 22–29 dc (8 rnds)

Rnd 30 dc2, (dc2tog) twice, dc19, (dc2tog) twice, dc17 (42)

Rnd 31 dc2, (dc2tog) twice, dc17, (dc2tog) twice, dc15 (38)

Rnd 32 dc1, (dc2tog) twice, dc15, (dc2tog) twice, dc14 (34)

Rnd 33 (dc2tog) twice, dc13, (dc2tog) twice, dc13 (30)

Rnd 34 (dc2tog) twice, dc11, (dc2tog) twice, dc11 (26)

Rnd 35 dc2tog, dc11, dc2tog, dc11 (24)

Rnd 36 dc2tog, dc10, dc2tog, dc10 (22)

Rnd 37 dc2tog, dc9, dc2tog, dc9 (20)

Rnd 38 dc

Fold flat and dc through both sides to close.

LEGS (make two)

Working in Magenta

Begin by dc6 into ring

Rnd 1 (dc2 into next st) 6 times (12)

Rnd 2 (dc1, dc2 into next st) 6 times (18)

Rnd 3 (dc2, dc2 into next st) 6 times (24)

Rnd 4 (dc3, dc2 into next st) 6 times (30)

Rnds 5–7 dc (3 rnds)

Rnd 8 (dc3, dc2tog) 3 times, dc15 (27)

Rnd 9 (dc2, dc2tog) 3 times, dc15 (24)

Rnd 10 (dc2tog) 12 times (12)

Rnds 11–18 dc (8 rnds)

ARMS (make two)

Working in Magenta

Begin by dc6 into ring

Rnd 1 (dc2 into next st) 6 times (12)

Rnd 2 (dc1, dc2 into next st) 6 times (18)

Rnd 3 (dc2, dc2 into next st) 6 times (24)

Rnds 4–8 dc (5 rnds)

Rnd 9 dc6, (dc1, dc2tog) 6 times (18)

Rnd 10 dc6, (dc2tog) 6 times (12)

Rnds 11–22 dc (12 rnds)

SEWING UP

1. Stuff BODY and join BASE to BODY with a round of dc from the top down in Magenta.

2. Sew LEAF into position on back of BODY with bottom approximately 18 rounds up from base.

3. Stuff feet and sew the top of LEGS flat, then sew into position onto joining edge of base.

4. Stuff hands and sew tops of ARMS flat perpendicular to hand, then sew into position on sides of BODY.

5. Embroider eyes with Black and Cream yarn.

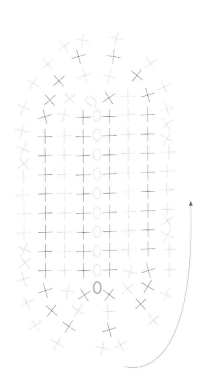

Brussels Sprout

A Christmas dinner essential – whether you love them or hate them, most of us manage to swallow a few of these every year. This is a great pattern to hook up as stocking-fillers for the whole family (especially those who would far prefer one with a smile than on the plate with their turkey).

BODY
The body is worked from the front to back.
Working in Chive
Begin by dc6 into ring
Rnd 1 (dc2 into next st) 6 times (12 sts)
Rnd 2 (dc1, dc2 into next st) 6 times (18)
Rnd 3 (dc2, dc2 into next st) 6 times (24)
Rnd 4 (dc3, dc2 into next st) 6 times (30)
Rnd 5 (dc4, dc2 into next st) 6 times (36)
Rnd 6 dc
Rnd 7 (dc5, dc2 into next st) 6 times (42)
Rnds 8–9 dc (2 rnds)
Rnd 10 (dc6, dc2 into next st) 6 times (48)
Rnds 11–16 dc (6 rnds)
Rnd 17 (dc2tog, dc6) 6 times (42)
Rnd 18 dc
Rnd 19 (dc2tog, dc5) 6 times (36)
Rnd 20 dc
Rnd 21 (dc2tog, dc4) 6 times (30)
Rnd 22 (dc2tog, dc3) 6 times (24)
Rnd 23 (dc2tog, dc2) 6 times (18)
Rnd 24 (dc2tog) 9 times (9)

LEAVES (make four)
Working in Kale
Begin by dc6 into ring
Rnd 1 (dc2 into next st) 6 times (12)
Rnd 2 (dc1, dc2 into next st) 6 times (18)
Rnd 3 (dc2, dc2 into next st) 6 times (24)

Rnd 4 (dc3, dc2 into next st) 6 times (30)
Rnd 5 (dc4, dc2 into next st) 6 times (36)
Rnd 6 (dc5, dc2 into next st) 6 times (42)
Change to Chive
Rnd 7 (dc6, dc2 into next st) 6 times (48)
Change to Kale
Rnd 8 dc12, (dc2 into next st) 36 times (84)
Break yarn.

LEGS (make two)
Working in Chive
Begin by dc6 into ring
Rnd 1 (dc2 into next st) 6 times (12)
Rnd 2 (dc1, dc2 into next st) 6 times (18)
Rnds 3–5 dc (3 rnds)
Rnd 6 (dc2tog) 6 times, dc6 (12)
Rnd 7 (dc2tog) 3 times, dc6 (9)
Rnds 8–13 dc (6 rnds)

Continues overleaf

MADE IN Chive and Kale (overleaf in Lime and Green)
YARN QUANTITIES 25g Body, 25g Leaves
TIME TO GROW Quick
REQUIRES Colour change

SEWING UP

1. Stuff BODY and gather final stitches to close, leaving a long end for sewing up.
2. Make two pairs of LEAVES as follows. Attach two LEAVES together by dc6 though both along non-increased edges. Repeat for second pair.
3. Place one pair of LEAVES onto back of BODY (decrease end) and sew around Lime colour change round to sew into position.
4. Sew second pair of LEAVES in the same way in the opposite direction to previous pair.
5. Stuff feet and sew tops of LEGS flat perpendicular to foot, then sew into position on bottom of BODY, on top of LEAVES.
6. Embroider eyes with Black and Cream yarn, and mouth with Black yarn.

Sewing up

Pumpkin

Aubergine

Butternut Squash

Broccoli

Cabbage

Bell Pepper

Cauliflower

Onion

Artichoke

Turnip

Garlic

Beetroot

Radish

Peas in a Pod

Baby Cucumber

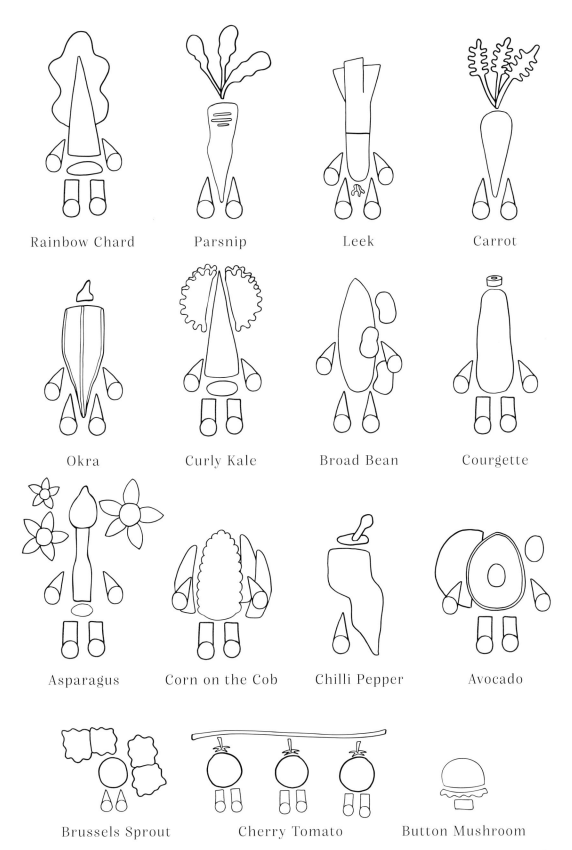

Rainbow Chard

Parsnip

Leek

Carrot

Okra

Curly Kale

Broad Bean

Courgette

Asparagus

Corn on the Cob

Chilli Pepper

Avocado

Brussels Sprout

Cherry Tomato

Button Mushroom

Know your veggies

Hiding inside this book are quite a few 'vegetables' that are botanically classified as fruits, alongside all the other edible parts of a plant. Fruits contain seeds and develop from a flower, so technically the tomato, pumpkin, squash, peas and peppers are all fruits, whereas the broccoli is actually a flower bud, and the Brussels sprout is a leaf!

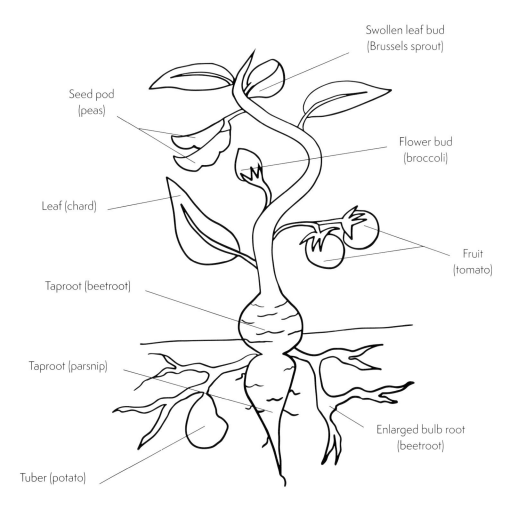

Swollen leaf bud
(Brussels sprout)

Seed pod
(peas)

Flower bud
(broccoli)

Leaf (chard)

Fruit
(tomato)

Taproot (beetroot)

Taproot (parsnip)

Enlarged bulb root
(beetroot)

Tuber (potato)

JOIN THE COMMUNITY

Share your vegetable pictures with the TOFT community using #alexsgarden and #croyourown. If you need any help with the techniques in this book, get in touch @toft_uk and we'll point you in the direction of a video that will ensure you get your vegetables to bloom as boldly as the ones on these pages.

TOFT's crochet range extends well beyond the fence at the bottom of the garden, and you can find more plant kits, subscriptions and information about events on our social media pages.

For all materials and tools, and to see our worldwide yarn stockists, visit www.toftuk.com

Thanks

My thanks begin this time with Edward and Alex. Ever since the day I let others know I was pregnant, I've been asked, 'What will you make for Alex?', and I really didn't know the answer until the first UK COVID-19 lockdown of 2020. Without their strength and continuous giggling, despite the uncertainty and challenges around them, this book would never have been made and I would never have found the love of another hobby. Over the last few years we've made some brilliant memories in our garden, and I know that mud, manure and mulching are now part of our lives forever. With further thanks to Farah for jumping on board and then taking it to the next level with her expertise on perfect edges, rye grass and rear rollers, and our shared pursuit of the perfect English country garden.

Of course, as this project developed over a long stretch of time, many hooks were involved, reworking the vegetables in as many colours as we could imagine.

Special thanks to:

Rachel Critchley for her expertise and attention to detail in checking all the technical details of what is my most diverse collection of patterns to date. For her tireless quest (with the help of Jess Leese) for the best deep purples, and for making sure the TOFT warehouse is full to the brim with Green for evermore.

Evie Birch for her step-by-step illustrations of all the techniques.

Further thanks to the whole TOFT team past and present, without whom none of this would be possible, but specifically:

Beth Plumbley for being ever enthusiastic about vegetable patches, and for the stamina involved in making the photos in this book so beautiful.

Natasha Jackson for never tiring of the request for 'just eight more like that', and for bringing a smile to every challenge, no matter how many legs it means making!

A big thanks to the extra-speedy hooks of Jess Leese, Annabel Cox, Connie Broadhead and Lillia Bowsher.

Photography was by Yantra Taneva and Rosie Collins. A special thanks to Yantra for the wizardry and perseverance that ensured the photos captured TOFT yarn perfectly, and Rosie for her patience in creating the perfect charts and graphics for each and every leaf.

Lastly, Liz Kidner for the final eye for detail that brought everything together so perfectly.